PARADOXES

OF FAITH AND REASON

Shalina Stilley

En Route Books and Media, LLC
Saint Louis, MO

Make the time

En Route Books and Media, LLC
5705 Rhodes Avenue
St. Louis, MO 63109

Cover credit: Bette Echad

ISBN-13: 978-1-956715-54-5
Library of Congress Control Number: 9781956715545

TABLE OF CONTENTS

To my students and all who grapple with paradox

ACKNOWLEDGMENTS

I am deeply grateful for all those who provided me with encouragement and feedback while working on this project. I would especially like to acknowledge my family, Allison McCord, Jerry Geurn, Cherie Peacock, Fr. Samuel Fontana, Fr. Albert Bruecken, Dr. Ronda Chervin, Dr. Sebastian Mahfood, OP, and Tati Rosenborg.

PART I

INTRODUCTION

PARADOX

Faith and reason are like two wings on which the human spirit rises to the contemplation of truth; and God has placed in the human heart a desire to know the truth—in a word, to know himself—so that, by knowing and loving God, men and women may also come to the fullness of truth about themselves. (*Fides et Ratio*, Introduction)

Paradox is at the very heart of the Gospel message. The Trinity, the Incarnation, the Cross and Resurrection, and the problem of evil are but a few examples of paradoxes of faith and reason. How can God be three in one? How can God be man? How can Jesus who is "the life" die on a Cross? How can we hold that God exists and is good when there is so much suffering in the world? All of these are questions which can cause the would-be Catholic to reject the faith and even the most devout of Catholics to stumble into perplexity.

By nature, we are rational and inquisitive beings who desire to know. If an orange elf were to suddenly appear next to you, you would rightly be curious. "Is it an optical illusion? Is it a hologram? Am I dreaming? Am I losing my mind?" All of these would be natural to ask.

Though some of the precepts of Catholicism can be known through reason, unaided by faith and revelation, many of them cannot be. One may be convinced by philosophical argument, for example, that there is a God—in the sense that there is a necessary being that does not depend on anything else for its existence. Yet philosophical arguments, even at their best, cannot prove all the precepts of the faith. They cannot, for example, prove that God is Trinitarian or that Christ is the second person of the Trinity. So, we are left with an important question: How can we be true to our rational nature and still have faith?

It might seem, at least at first glance, that we have only two options: to be rational and to dismiss beliefs that cannot be proved to be true through reason alone; or to be irrational, but faithful, and accept such beliefs. To be true to our nature, to be fully rational, would seem to require rejecting many of the precepts of the Catholic faith. To be true to the faith, on the other hand, would seem to require acting contrary to our rational nature by accepting precepts that seem absurd. Shall we be fully human and rational but non-Catholic, or shall we be Catholic but not fully rational?

Many have chosen the first option and embraced atheism or agnosticism. Many others have chosen the second and embraced fideism. Luckily though, there is a third option. It is possible to be a rational *and* Catholic. This third option is not the easiest—as it can require wading through paradox by way of persistent and courageous inquiry—but it is by far the best insofar as it can bring us to a deeper understanding of the truth.

What is a paradox?

For our purposes here, I will use the term *paradox* to mean *a set of beliefs, claims, ideas, concepts, or statements which seem to be contradictory but which in actuality are not.* An obvious example within the realm of theology is the paradox of the Trinity. It seems contradictory and indeed absurd to claim that God is one and that God is Trinitarian. Another is the paradox of the Cross. God the Father is good—nay, even goodness itself—yet he allows his own Son to suffer an excruciating death. Huh?

An example within the realm of philosophy can be found in Plato's dialogue *Meno*. Socrates, in his typical Socratic fashion, asks Meno a series of questions. At first, Meno thinks he knows the answers. "Ah ha!" he thinks to himself. "This is easy! Socrates is not living up to his reputation of being a gadfly." But after further inquiry from Socrates, he comes to realize that what he was so certain of before is now as misty as ever. All he comes to be certain of is that what he though was right is not at all right. This in turn leads poor Meno headlong into the iceberg which has come to be known as the learner's paradox.

A paradox, whether it is theological or philosophical, is similar to a mystery. The word "mystery" is derived from the Latin word *mysterium* which can be translated as mystery, mystic, hidden, or religious. A paradox is similar to a mystery insofar as it is something which is hidden. A paradox is "in the mist," so to speak. Though a paradox is not easy to grasp, it is in principle knowable. Though I may only see a general outline of a ship in the mist, the ship and its qualities are in principle knowable. Likewise, though I may not know what is behind a veil—be it the veil of the holy of holies, the veil of a tabernacle, or some other veil—it does not necessarily follow that I can never come to know what is behind the veil.

Let us return to Meno. Though it is true that the poor man wrecked his ship upon the learner's paradox, it is also true that it did him a great deal of good. It enabled him to know what he didn't know, and it thereby instilled in him the desire and ability to begin true inquiry. Instead of saying, "I know the answer, and we are now finished," he came to say, "I don't know the answer, I have no idea how to find the answer, and I have no idea if it is even possible to find the answer, but I desire to know." Through grappling with paradox, he became intellectually humble.

Stages of Growth

There is a parallel between what Meno experienced and what people may experience in their spiritual or intellectual journey. Here are the stages:

1. Stage of Certitude: "I know the answer."

2. Stage of Perplexity: "Wait, I thought I knew the answer but now I realize I don't."

3. Stage of Paradox: "I don't know the answer, but I am willing to learn."

Stage of Certitude: At the outset, many people who are inquiring about the existence of God, the truth or falsity of religion, and the meaning of life think they know the answer. An atheist may reason thus: "If there was a God and if he, she, or it was good, there would be no suffering in the world. Since there is suffering in the world, it is evident that there is no God." The atheist believes, without further ado, that there is no God. Yet in a sense he has faith that there is no God as he has not yet truly considered alternative possibilities. More specifically, he has not yet considered that, although there is suffering in the world, there may be a reason why a good God would allow such suffering. In his mind, it is a contradiction—not a mere paradox—to hold both that a good God exists and that there is suffering in the world. He is not perplexed about things; he is certain.

At this stage, the Christian, too, has not reached a state of perplexity. He may reason thus, "God said it, I believe it, that settles it." At this stage, the individual may think he knows the answer (and indeed he may), but he is still in the realm of fideism and has not yet plunged into perplexity. He believes in the existence of God but has not yet grappled with the mystery of God, and he may have a very simplistic understanding of God. He cannot yet provide a reason for his hope. (cf. 1 Peter 3:15-16) As a consequence, when tribulations and temptations overwhelm him, his faith may very well fade into the background, or he may experience a crisis of faith. This crisis in turn may lead him to turn to atheism as a quick and easy answer.

Stage of Perplexity: At this stage, the individual comes to have humility in the face of mystery. Rather than having standard, pat, carefully boxed answers, he recognizes that he doesn't know what he thought he knew. He is now ready for authentic inquiry. The atheist may think: "Though I thought I knew there was no God, I now realize that there may be. Though I thought it was impossible for a good God to allow suffering, I now realize that there may be a reason a good God might allow suffering. What I once thought was a contradiction may be a paradox which I have not yet looked at honestly."

The Christian, at this stage, may reason thus, "I thought I knew exactly who God is but now I realize that there is a great deal of mystery. I don't know where God is when my loved ones and I suffer. Sometimes I cry out, 'my God, my God, why have you abandoned me?' And, sometimes, I wonder if God is even there. Oh, me of little faith!"

At the stage of perplexity, one is at a crossroad and many options lay before him (regardless of whether he is an atheist or a Christian). Rather than continuing to face his uncertainty, the atheist may embrace agnosticism without further ado. He is in a better position than before, given that now he is able to be honest with himself about his own ignorance. Yet an apathy may set in and lead him to abandon the search for truth and understanding altogether. Likewise, he may settle with skepticism and relativism.

The Christian at this stage may likewise embrace agnosticism or even atheism. Rather than acknowledging that he doesn't know exactly who God is, but that it may be possible to come to know, he may settle for the easy answer, "There is no God." Or he may settle for, "It's impossible to know anything."

Stage of Paradox. Those who endure the stage of perplexity without falling into apathy, skepticism, or relativism, enter into the stage of paradox. This is the stage where true growth and transformation occurs. The former atheist will begin to look for answers to his perplexities. Rather than say, "I know there is no God" he will say, "I don't know how to reconcile the notion of a good God with the fact that there is suffering in the world, but I will try to find a way to reach such reconciliation."

The Christian, too, will begin to look for answers to his perplexities and will be in a position to grow in wisdom, understanding, faith, and love of God. In his prayer life, he may turn to God in humility, saying, "Lord, show me your truth." Or he may say, "Speak Lord, your servant is listening." (1 Samuel 3:10) In his rational pursuits, he may begin to look more deeply into the precepts of his faith, seek to resolve apparent contradictions, and proceed with an open and receptive mind. He may also look to others who have had similar crises to learn how they grappled with perplexity. This stage is one of receptivity. The soul is primed to receive grace and insights. The mind is primed to receive understanding.

Of course, what I have provided above are mere examples of how one may journey through the stage of paradox. There is an abundance of other examples. The key element of this stage is a recognition that seeming contradictions may be mere paradoxes. When poor Meno entered into the stage of perplexity—and came to know that he didn't know— Socrates was elated. He knew Meno was making great progress at last! Meno then was able to enter into the stage of paradox and begin to attain wisdom. Rather than give up his search, saying, "It is futile to continue. Knowledge is impossible," he courageously dug in. In the end—though he didn't come to know everything—he was richly rewarded.

Goals and Guides

The goal of this book is to enter into the stage of paradox. It will entail looking at many precepts of the faith which seem to be contradictory, exploring them in greater depth, coming to a deeper understanding of them, and recognizing them as paradoxes rather than contradictions. I will call this *illumination* of paradoxes. The goal is not, however, to resolve all uncertainty or to obliterate the need for faith and ongoing receptivity to God. Such an endeavor would be foolish. Our goal, in short, is not to resolve paradoxes, but to illuminate them.

Before delving into specific paradoxes, a word should be said about guides. Meno's guide was Socrates. Socrates helped Meno to wade through his perplexity but, rather than abandon him, he guided him into the stage of paradox. When Meno recognized his own ignorance, Socrates helped him maintain hope rather than despair.

In our journey, we will also have guides. One of them will be Aquinas—a man of true courage and faith who did not turn a blind eye to apparent contradictions, nor enter into despair but dug in with a receptive mind and heart. He too had his own guides. He looked to Scripture, the Fathers of the Church, Aristotle, and others learned people. More importantly he looked to God as his primary guide, proceeding in a spirit of prayer and receptivity.

Another guide will be St. John of the Cross. He will guide us by his words but, more importantly, by his example. He was a man of true and authentic faith who never shied away from perplexity but entered into it with great hope. He allowed God to lead him into perplexity, or what he called "the dark night" and in the darkness he came to know God more deeply than he otherwise would have. He journeyed past idolatry, past thinking that God was a mere feeling or image, past relying on himself, and into recognition that God is far more than we can ever know of him.

Yet another guide will be St. Catherine of Siena. Like St. John of the Cross, she will guide us by her words and example. Her journey began not in the halls of a university but in the "cell of self-knowledge." Through years of solitude, she came to think of herself as "she who is not" and thereby came to know that God is "he who is." It is through temptation and trial, not through an arrogant certitude, that she came to know God. She did not shun paradox, she entered into it.

There will also be many other guides, and the most important one will be the Trinity. So, we do not journey alone, we journey with the Father, Son, Holy Spirit, and many great Saints and sages. Let us allow them to illuminate us as we journey through the stage of paradox. Let us begin.

PART II

THEOLOGICAL PARADOXES

PARADOX OF THE TRINITY

How can three be one? How can a *bona fide* monotheist believe in the Trinity? It seems that if oneness is true oneness, it cannot be three. Either something is one, authentically one, or it is not. Multiplicity is not singularity, nor is singularity multiplicity, nor e're could it be.

These musings lead us into the paradox and mystery of the Trinity which is one of the most difficult paradoxes to illuminate because the source of illumination of the Trinity is the Trinity itself. It is, as it were, a paradox of light that can only be illuminated by the light itself. What is being illuminated here is itself the source of all illumination. In light, we see light. (cf. Psalm 36:9)

So, grappling with this paradox of the Trinity requires staring into the brightest of bright lights. As such, it can be blinding. Instead of feeling that we are growing in knowledge, we can end up feeling that we are entering into complete ignorance, complete unknowing. It is no accident that mystics who enter into unity with God also experience darkness. Similarly, it is no accident that Plato compares the philosophical journey and attainment of wisdom to coming out of a cave and being blinded by the sun.

We cannot know God as he is in himself. To comprehend the Trinity would require becoming the Trinity. Nevertheless, there are methods for illuminating it and thereby establishing that there is no inherent contradiction in the doctrine of the Trinity. To be sure, the Trinity cannot be proven through reason alone. To attempt to do so would be foolish insofar as the Trinity *by nature* transcends us and our rational faculty. (cf. *Summa Theologica* I, 32, 1. Hereafter abbreviated *ST.*)

As will be discussed in greater detail in the section on Paradoxes of Reason, analogies can be useful when attempting to speak about God. They are likewise useful when establishing that the doctrine of the Trinity does not entail a contradiction. St. Patrick famously used the analogy of the shamrock. Given that a shamrock has three leaves but one nature, it is clear that it is possible for something to be three in a sense but one in another sense. The shamrock has one nature but three aspects. Others have used the analogy of the family. One family can include three persons: a father, a mother, and a child. Moreover, the child can be the result of the love between the father and the mother, which is analogous to the Holy Spirit being the love between the Father and the Son. Still others have used the more abstract analogy of the human mind. A human has intellect, memory, and will but is still one. We do not say that the intellect is a human, the memory another human, and the will yet another. A human has three faculties but is one person. Moreover, given that the human person has both intellect and will, he is capable of loving. As Aquinas points out, "in rational creatures, possessing intellect and will, there is found the representation of the Trinity by way of image, inasmuch as there is found in them the word conceived, and the love proceeding." (*ST* I, 45, 7)

Of all analogies, St. Augustine's is perhaps the best. As the ocean can never fit into a shell, or even oodles of shells, so, too, the Trinity can never fit into our small minds. Rather than despair, however, we should be grateful that we can have a glimpse of the magnificence of God. The ocean cannot fit into a shell, but shells can contain small traces of the ocean. Thanks be to God!

Analogies will never do justice to the Trinity given that there are also disanalogies. For example, the shamrock has three leaves and the human mind has three faculties; but neither the shamrock nor the mind are three persons. Nevertheless, analogies can at least give us reason to believe that the doctrine of the Trinity it is not inherently contradictory. The doctrine will forever be paradoxical given the smallness of our minds, but by the grace of God we can forever be drawn more deeply into a knowledge and love of the Trinity. The paradox will never be exhausted, but the mystery will—if we are receptive and humble—forever unveil itself to us.

St. Elizabeth of the Trinity, a Carmelite nun whose spiritual life centered on the Indwelling of the Trinity within her soul and who described the Trinity as an abyss, can be our guide. With her, we can pray, "Oh my Three, my All, my Beatitude, infinite Solitude, Immensity in which I lose myself, I surrender myself to You as Your prey. Bury Yourself in me that I may bury myself in You until I depart to contemplate

in Your light the abyss of Your greatness." (St. Elizabeth of
the Trinity, *Complete Works*, volume 1)

CHRISTOLOGICAL PARADOXES

This truth, which God reveals to us in Jesus Christ, is
not opposed to the truths which philosophy per-
ceives. (*Fides et Ratio* 34)

THE PARADOX OF THE INCARNATION

The paradox of the Incarnation is another huge paradox
of faith. How could God, who is the creator of the universe
and who stands outside time, become a human, that is, a created and temporally finite being? This seems to be a *bona fide*
contradiction if ever there was one! If God is the creator of
all, it would seem that he cannot also be created. If he is outside time, it would likewise seem that he cannot be inside
time.

The seeming contradiction about Christ being the creator and created can be illuminated by considering the nature
of change. Aquinas, borrowing from Aristotle, notes that
change entails a relation between two things and that it is
possible for one of the things to change without the other
one changing. (*ST* III, 16, 6) For example, two people can
stand next to each other and their relation in space can
change even if only one of them changes position. For

example, Tom could be standing to the left of Jane and Jane could move to the right of Tom without Tom himself changing his position. The resulting change in relation is a real change but is brought about by the motion of only one of the two people.

With this insight as a foundation, Aquinas then explains that when God became man, the change was on the part of man, not God. Aquinas states, "now to be man belongs to God by reason of the union, which is a relation. And hence to be man is newly predicated of God without any change in Him, by a change in the human nature.... And hence, when...God was made man, we understand no change on the part of God." (*ST* III, 16, 6 resp 2) Stated more simply, when Jesus became incarnate, he did not change insofar as he ceased to be God nor in the sense that he became a creature rather than creator, rather human nature changed with regard to its relation to God. Before the Incarnation, Jesus was God and therefore the creator. After the Incarnation, he was still God, and therefore the creator, but he was also united to human nature, his creation. Analogously, just as before Jane moved to the right of Tom, Tom was at position x, so, too, before the Incarnation, Jesus was the Creator. And just as after Jane moved a new position came about (even though Tom was still at position x) so, too, a new relation came about with regard to creation when Jesus became incarnate. He remained the creator but was united to his creation in a new way.

The seeming contradiction about God being both out-side and inside time can be illuminated in a similar way. Christ proclaims that he is the "Alpha and the Omega… who is, who was, and who is to come." (Rev 1:8) In saying this, his claim is *not*, "I am the Alpha and the Omega but not also the Beta, Gamma, Delta, and so on." He claims to be *all* of it. Similarly, his claim is not, "I am not in the past, present, or future." He claims to be *in all* of it. It is not a contradiction to say that God is outside time but also inside it. He is beyond his creation, but he is also inside it (though he is not reduci-ble to it). Furthermore, it is "in him [that] all things hold to-gether." (Col 1:15-17) So, rather than say that God is outside time, and hence cannot be inside it, we can say that time is inside God.

Another aspect of the paradox of the Incarnation hinges on the question: Why would God, the creator of the universe, become one of us? Our creator becoming one of us is not akin to one of us becoming a chimp, or a rabbit, or even a cockroach. All analogy breaks down here. There is no anal-ogy that can adequately capture the profound humility and love of God. Were we to choose to become cockroaches out of a desire to transform them and make them human-like, even this would require far less humility and love than for God to become man.

So why would God choose to become one of us? The an-swer is love. He became one of us not because he had to but because of his goodness. Borrowing from Pseudo-Dionysius,

Aquinas says, "it belongs to the essence of goodness to communicate itself to others…. Hence it is manifest that it was
fitting that God should become incarnate." (*ST* III,1,1) Insofar as God is God and his dignity far surpasses that of creatures, it is not fitting that God should become man. Nevertheless, insofar as God is love, it is very fitting. (cf. *ST* III, 1,1,
resp obj 2) God loves us so much, and wants so much for us
to be united to him, that he has become united to us. Though
we do not merit being united to him, he has given us this
union gratuitously.

The mystery of the humility of Jesus is another aspect of
this paradox. "Though [Jesus] was in the form of God, [he]
did not regard equality with God something to be grasped.
Rather, he emptied himself, taking the form of a slave, coming in human likeness; and found human in appearance, he
humbled himself, becoming obedient to death, even death
on a cross." (Phil 2: 6-8) In becoming one of us, he exalted
us, but humbled himself. His love for us and his humility are
two sides of the same coin.

Jesus is the epitome and prime example of humility. The
term "humility" is derived from *humus* (which means *earth*
or *ground*) and so can be translated as "from the earth" or
"grounded." The God of all became a baby, born in a barn,
among the earthly hay and stinky farm animals. Now, that is
true humility!

The mystery of the poverty of Jesus is yet another aspect
part of the paradox of the Incarnation given that poverty is

part of the humility of Jesus. Though, "all things were created through him and for him," he became poor and homeless with nothing to wear but swaddling clothes. (Colossians 1:16) As Jesus himself puts it, "Foxes have dens and birds of the sky have nests, but the Son of Man has nowhere to rest his head." (Mat 8:20) Here again, analogy is insufficient for expressing the profundity of this paradox. Even if the wealthiest non-divine person alive were to give up all he had, give it to the poor, and become destitute out of love, this would not compare to what Jesus did. Even the wealthiest of non-divine persons is still a creature of God and hence a recipient of God's wealth, not a creator of it. Moreover, even the wealthiest of persons is less wealthy than God. God's love so far surpasses us that it cannot be fully comprehended. "'What eye has not seen, and ear has not heard, and what has not entered the human heart, what God has prepared for those who love him,' this God has revealed to us through the Spirit." (1 Cor, 2: 9. Is 64:3)

What the humility and poverty of Jesus shows us is that he loves us more than we can possibly imagine and that, if we wish to imitate him, we too must pour out our lives through love. So, once again, God reveals himself to us in paradox and thereby invites us to enter into it ourselves. It is by entering into it, rather than shunning it or concluding that it is contradictory, that we can come to a deeper understanding of who God is.

THE PARADOX OF THE BRIDEGROOM

Another Christological paradox is that Jesus is a bridegroom. Throughout Scripture and tradition, God is spoken of as a bridegroom. In the Old Testament, we read, "for the LORD delights in you, and your land shall be espoused. For as a young man marries a virgin, your Builder shall marry you; and as a bridegroom rejoices in his bride so shall your God rejoice in you. (Isaiah 62: 4-5). Similarly, in Hosea we read, "I will betroth you to me forever: I will betroth you to me with justice and with judgment, with loyalty and with compassion; I will betroth you to me with fidelity." (Hosea 2:21-22) Also, in the *Song of Songs*, we are given a beautiful love poem which many of the Saints have interpreted as an image of the love that the Bride (the Church) has for Christ the Bridegroom.

In the New Testament, Jesus refers to himself as a bridegroom. When the disciples of John the Baptist saw that Christ's followers did not fast but that the Pharisees did, they were perplexed. In response, Jesus said, "the attendants of the bridegroom cannot mourn as long as the bridegroom is with them, can they? But the days will come when the bridegroom is taken away from them, and then they will fast." (Mat 9:14-15; cf. Mark 2:18-20 and Luke 5:33-35) When John the Baptist was asked if he was the Messiah, he responded by claiming to be the friend of Christ, the bridegroom. He said, "it is the bridegroom who has the bride; and yet the bridegroom's friend, who stands there and listens to him, is filled with joy at the bridegroom's voice." (John 3:29)

In addition to many passages in scripture which refer to Christ as a bridegroom, the Church herself has a long tradition of seeing herself as the Bride of Christ. For example, in the Rite of Consecration of Virgins, the Bishop says, "the Church is the Bride of Christ." Addressing the candidates for consecration, he says, "you are a sign of the great mystery of salvation, proclaimed at the beginning of human history and fulfilled in the marriage covenant between Christ and his Church." The Rite also describes the consecrated virgin as "a transcendent sign of the Church's love for Christ, and an eschatological image of this heavenly Bride of Christ and the life to come." (*Ordo Consecrationis Virginum.* See also: *Catechism of the Catholic Church*, 924)

It is a great mystery and paradox that Christ not only becomes one of us but even becomes the Bridegroom of the Church. It seems crazy that God would want to be espoused to his own creatures. To some, it may even seem scandalous, blasphemous, and idolatrous—especially if we think of marriage in a secular, non-sacramental way.

One way to illuminate this paradox is to look at what marriage is in a sacramental sense. Ideally, sacramental marriage is unitive, self-transcendent, procreative, free, and founded on love. Though marriage is a profound theological topic, which can only be fully understood with the help of faith, philosophy can help us understand its nature. More specifically, Aristotle's insights on true friendship—as opposed to merely incidental friendship—can help us.

In his treatise on friendship in *Nicomachean Ethics*, Aristotle starts by looking at the end or goal of friendship. Some friendship has pleasure as its end. A classic example of this is friendship based on a desire for one's own pleasure or, to use contemporary terminology, "friends with benefits." If asked, "Why are you in a relationship with this person?" the response would be, "Because she brings me pleasure." The problem with this type of friendship, however, is that it is short-lived. Once the "friend" is no longer pleasant—perhaps because she becomes old, unattractive, a shrew, or a bore—the relationship ceases. Such a friendship is not authentic, according to Aristotle, because it is based on a desire for *one's own* good rather than the good of the *other*. Moreover, this type of friendship is not necessarily even based on one's authentic desires—it may be based on merely apparent goods.[1]

Another type of friendship is based on utility. Aristotle claims that this type is frequently found among older people who need the help of others. He also gives the example of host and guest relationships. If the friend is useful, the friendship endures, but as soon as he is no longer useful, it ends. Like pleasure-based friendship, one desires his own good rather than that of the other. For this reason, Aristotle

---

[1] See *Nicomachean Ethics,* Books VIII and IX.

concludes that it is not an authentic friendship and that, like friendship of pleasure, it is short-lived. As long as the friend is useful, the relationship endures, but as soon as the friend is not, it ends. Also, like the friendship of pleasure, this type of friendship is not necessarily based on one's authentic desires.

The third type of friendship Aristotle discusses is authentic friendship. Friendship is only authentic when the goal is the good of the *other* person. The true friend must be good or virtuous *himself*, he must be good *for* the other person, and there must be a certain amount of equality or similarity between the two. If the friends are not good or virtuous *themselves*, they will not be good *for* each other.

It should be noted that authentic friendship is not antithetical to pleasure and utility. When two people wish the true good of the other, are themselves good, and are good *for* each other, they may incidentally be useful and pleasant to each other. The difference though is that pleasure and utility are neither the goal nor the foundation of the friendship. Even if the other is no longer useful or pleasant, the relationship endures because it is not based on passing things, selfishness, or self-centeredness, but on self-transcendent love.

Authentic friendship is the foundation of a healthy sacramental marriage. The spouses must be good themselves, good *for* the other, and will the authentic good of the other. Aquinas's definition of charity as a desire for the true good of the other echoes Aristotle's description of true friendship. Marriage in a sacramental sense entails and fosters charity.

Within this context, it becomes clear that Jesus is the bridegroom and the Church is the bride specifically in the sense that his relationship with us is based on authentic friendship. Jesus tells us, "I will not now call you servants... but my friends." (John 15:15) Mystical espousal to Christ is akin to true friendship insofar as Christ is good himself, good for us, and wills our true good. He does not espouse himself to his us (his Church) because we are useful or pleasant to him but simply because he loves us. He the most authentic bridegroom there ever could be.

Grappling with this paradox can lead us to a deeper understanding of Christ, and it can also lead us to a deeper understanding of what he has called us to be. He is the bridegroom, and we are therefore called to enter into this mystical marriage by loving him in return. This entails becoming good and virtuous, being a good for others, willing the true good of others, and loving God and others for their own sake rather than for our sake.

Acquiring this perfect love requires grace and purification of our ulterior motives. Many of the mystics teach us that this happens through a series of desolations and consolations. Theologians sometimes refer to the stages of this purification as *purgative, illuminative,* and *unitive.* Each stage involves growing in virtue and becoming more and more detached from sin.

Generally speaking, the purgative stage involves being purged of attachment to mortal sin, passions, and evil inclinations. The illuminative stage involves being purged of attachment to venial sin and continued grown in virtue. The unitive stage—wherein mystical espousal takes place—entails having perfect charity or, in other words, perfect friendship with God. The soul in this state loves God and others in a pure and selfless way—without being motivated by a desire for spiritual consolations or a heavenly reward. Put more simply, it involves loving the other without being motivated by pleasure or utility.[2]

In *The Dialogue*, Catherine of Siena speaks of this purification. God the Father reveals to her that there are various types of tears that people shed on the way to perfection. Some tears are shed by those who recognize their sinfulness and weep out of fear of punishment from God. These souls approach God out of fear, and they desire a relationship with him only because they believe it will be useful in avoiding punishment. Another type of tears is shed by those who are in a period of desolation and desire for spiritual consolations (or, in other words, by those who want something from God). Another type is shed by those who have begun to conform their wills to God and hence have reached a sort of self-transcendence. And yet another type of tears is shed by those

---

[2] Devine, Arthur. "State or Way (Purgative, Illuminative, Unitive)." The Catholic Encyclopedia. Vol. 14.

who are united with God and are perfect in charity.[3] Souls
who shed this last type of tears recognize that there is nothing they have done, or ever could do, to merit God's love.
They also recognize that to love God with the same love that
he loves them, they must love their neighbor, "without any
concern for [their] own spiritual or material profit."[4] Those
with perfect charity are those who love purely and selflessly.

In wading through this paradox, we may wonder why are
we called to perfect charity and espousal with the Bridegroom. The answer is that he has first loved us with perfect
charity and espoused himself to us. This truth is revealed to
us through his pierced Sacred Heart. St. Catherine asks Jesus
why he allowed his side to be pierced and blood and water to
pour forth. He responds, "There were plenty of reasons, but
I shall tell you one of the chief. My longing for humankind
was infinite but the actual deed of bearing pain and torment
was finite and could never show all the love I had. This is why
I wanted you to see my inmost heart, so that you would see
that I loved you more than finite suffering could show."[5]
This response illuminates the mystery of his espousal by
showing us that Christ loves us in a purely self-less way. He
does not need us and indeed, "our praise adds nothing to

---

[3]Catherine, of Siena. *The Dialogue*. (New York: Paulist Press,
1980), sections 88-90.

[4] Ibid., section 89.

[5] Ibid., Section 75.

[his] greatness." (*Roman Missal*) Nor is he motivated by pleasure —there is nothing pleasurable about crucifixion. Jesus is motivated by pure, self-transcendent, infinite love; and it is with this love that he espouses himself to souls.

This mystical espousal of Jesus to his people is not a mere symbol, as is ordinary marriage. Ordinary marriage (or marriage between two non-divine humans) is a sacrament in that it is a sign. Mystical espousal, however, is the reality which marriage signifies and is far more than a sign. Likewise, the Consecrated Virgin is a "sign" in that she is a reminder to the Church that we are all called to union with Christ.

So, the paradox of Christ's espousal is illuminated by looking at the nature of this union. It is a union of the soul's will with that of Christ's, and it pours forth into perfect love for God and neighbor. Illumination of this paradox can in turn illuminate the paradox of the Incarnation by showing us why God became one of us: to unite himself to us in perfect love. It is common for illumination of one paradox to illuminate others.

PARADOXES IN THE EARTHLY LIFE OF JESUS

Many paradoxes can be found in Jesus' earthly life, ministry, and preaching. Here we will explore three: the paradox of Jesus' anger, the paradox of hate, and the paradox of the cross and resurrection.

Paradox of Anger

Jesus is often portrayed as a warm, fuzzy, meek, and gentle lamb whose heart is full of mercy; and yet we hear him say, "Get behind me Satan!" and "Depart from me you evildoers into the eternal fire!" (Mt 16:23; Mt 25:41) We also see him whip through the temple, condemning thieves and turning over money-changers' tables. (Jn 2:15). It is no surprise that these scenes from the life of Jesus are seldom if ever portrayed in icons. Perhaps these scenes are thought to be too perplexing or paradoxical to portray. We prefer serene pictures of the Sacred Heart and the Divine Mercy. Yet, perhaps this is unfortunate since they alone do not reveal all aspects of the nature of God's love.

Inordinate anger is one of the seven deadly sins and indeed blatantly clashes with the merciful, Sacred Heart. The key word here, though, is "inordinate." An example of inordinate anger is a desire for vengeance which is unreasonable given the nature of the offence that provokes the anger. If one were to become unhinged at something very minor or show vengeance against someone who does not deserve it, such would be inordinate, and therefore sinful. In other words, as Aquinas teaches us, too much anger given the circumstances or too fierce a response to feelings of anger can be contrary to charity and even in some cases mortally sinful. (ST II-II, 158, 3)

Though inordinate anger is indeed sinful and clashes with the Sacred Heart, there is a type of anger which is actually praiseworthy and in accord with charity. This is sometimes called righteous or zealous anger. In his discussion of anger, Aquinas maintains that anger can be properly ordered if it is motivated by the desire to maintain justice or correct injustice. (*ST* II-II, 158, obj. 3) Thus, not only is standing by idly while someone is being exploited not a virtue, it can in some circumstances be a vice.

Looking at the context of the passages in which Jesus displays anger, it is clear that his anger was ordinate, not inordinate. In the temple, he was trying to put an end to the financial exploitation of those who had come to worship. He was trying to correct the unjust and get them to stop robbing people, not randomly punishing the innocent.

Similarly, when looking at the context of the passage in which Jesus says, "Get behind me Satan!" it is clear that his anger toward Peter was ordinate, not inordinate. After saying, "Get behind me Satan!" he adds, "you are a hindrance to me, for you are not on the side of God but of men." (Matthew 16: 23) Jesus is correcting Peter and trying to get him to stop resisting the will of God, not seeking random vengeance.

Again, when we hear Jesus say, "Depart from me you accursed, into the eternal fire." (Matthew 25:41) But important to consider the context. Three things are particularly noteworthy about this passage. First, Jesus is speaking hypothetically. He is telling his listeners what he *will* say to them *if* they ignore their brothers and sisters who are hungry, naked, sick, or in prison. It is a warning, not an inordinate expression of anger or desire for vengeance. Second, Jesus is likely trying to prevent injustice, and correct indifference and apathy, by admonishing us to be attentive to the needs of his little ones, his dear anawim. Thirdly, he is showing us that in order to have authentic love for God we must have authentic love for others. "Truly I say to you, as you did it to the least of these my brethren, you did it to me." (Matthew 25:40)

One of the insights we can gain from considering the paradox of Jesus' anger is that three questions should be asked when attempting to establish whether anger is inordinate. First, *Is the anger warranted given the situation?* Second, *Is the anger expressed in a reasonable manner given the situation?* And third, *Is the motive of the angry person to prevent and to correct injustice?* If the answer to all these questions is "yes," the anger is praiseworthy.

Let us look at these questions in the context of the scenario of Jesus in the temple.

First question: *Is the anger of Jesus warranted given the situation?*

Answer: Yes, given that the men in the temple were thieves, robbing worshipers of their hard-earned money, Jesus' anger was warranted. If Jesus not been angry about this injustice and exploitation, or if he had done nothing about it, he would have been negligent. It would have been a lack of charity to do nothing. So, yes, it was warranted given the situation.

Second question: *Is Jesus' anger expressed in a reasonable manner?*

Answer: In this situation, Jesus did not use inordinate force. He did not, for example, assault the money changers or even take the money they had stolen. He did the minimum necessary, it would seem, to stop the exploitation and make his point. Without tables, the exploiters were no longer in a position to continue exploiting. So, yes, it was expressed in a reasonable manner.

Third question: *Is the motive of Jesus to prevent and correct injustice?*

Answer: Obviously, we cannot know all of the motives of the Heart of Jesus, but he does give us an indication of his motive when he says, "You are turning my Father's house into a den of thieves." Given this statement, it seems that at least in part his motive was to correct injustice and prevent further exploitation of those who were trying to render honor to God. So, yes, his goal was to prevent and correct injustice.

Now let us compare this scenario with that of another in which Buster enters a tavern and sees Ramblin' Bob winking at his girlfriend Susie. In this scenario, Buster approaches

Bob, turns over his table, punches him in the face (thereby knocking out a tooth), and threatens to kill him if he ever sees him so much as look at Susie again.

First question: *Is the anger of Buster warranted given the situation?*

Answer: In this scenario, Buster's anger does not seem to be warranted given that Ramblin' Bob was merely winking at his girlfriend.

Second question: *Is Buster's anger expressed in a reasonable manner?*

Answer: No. A wink should not be punished by a punch in the face and a lost tooth.

Third question: *Is the motive of Buster to prevent and correct injustice?*

Answer: No. In this scenario, Buster's motive is not to try to prevent or correct the injustice of marital infidelity. (Bob and Susie are neither married nor engaged). Nor is his motive to try to protect Susie. (Ramblin' Bob was winking at Susie, not assaulting her). Rather, Buster's motive is to seek vengeance for what is at worst a minor offense. (Who knows, maybe Ramblin' Bob was only winking at Susie because, right before Buster walked in the door, she had told him how much she loves Buster.)

Anger is frequently condemned as sinful even when it is not—which is no surprise given that anger is categorized as one of the seven deadly sins and given that anger is often expressed inordinately. But to categorize all anger as sinful (like Buster's) is to miss a very important nuance, one which Jesus illustrates through his words and actions. If one has Christ-like anger, one should be grateful for it. It is a grace. The paradox of Jesus' anger thus sheds great light on the nature of charity and its relation to anger. We are called to be angry in the face of injustice, not apathetic and negligent. Though anger is often inordinate, in many circumstances it is actually virtuous.

Paradox of Hate

Similar to the paradox of anger is the paradox of hate and discord. Numerous passages in the Gospels portray Jesus' proclaiming that he has come to bring division and telling his disciples that they must hate their lives. Here are a few:

> "If any one comes to me without hating his father and mother, wife and children, brothers and sisters, and even his own life, he cannot be my disciple." (Lk 14:26)

> "Do not think that I have come to bring peace upon the earth. I have come to bring not peace but

the sword. For I have come to set a man 'against his father, a daughter against her mother, and a daughter-in-law against her mother-in-law; and one's enemies will be those of his household.' (Mt 10:34-36)

Whoever loves his life loses it, and whoever hates his life in this world will preserve it for eternal life. (John 12:25)

"Whoever finds his life will lose it, and whoever loses his life for my sake will find it." (Mt. 10:39)

Were one to open Scripture, knowing nothing about it, and land on any of these passages, he would likely think that he was reading the words of a madman. This Jesus speaks of discord, the sword, losing one's life, and hating the world and one's family members. He sounds more like a demon than the Incarnation of love.

One way to illuminate this is to make a distinction between two types of hate. The first type is incompatible with charity. To hate in this sense is to fail to will the true good of the other. For example, Buster could hate Bob in the sense that he wishes him evil.

The second type of hate entails a detachment from worldly or false goods and is compatible with charity. An example is fasting. One might fast and in this sense hate steak, but such "hate" would stem from virtue (such as temperance, piety, and a desire to put God first and created things second). Similarly, one might hate life in the sense that she desires more to be with God than to be immersed in things of the world. It is not that she hates life in the sense that she is ungrateful for it, or in the sense that she thinks it is evil, but in the sense that she desires an even higher life— one in which she is free from desires that keep her clinging to things less than God.

If we use the term "hate" in this second sense, Jesus' words make sense. They are still paradoxical, but they do not imply a contradiction. Again, Jesus says, "Whoever loves his life loses it, and whoever hates his life in this world will preserve it for eternal life." (John 12:25) This can be read as, "Whoever hates his life, in the same sense that he hates steak when he is fasting, will preserve it for eternal life." Adding nuances, this can also be read as, "Whoever prefers to cling to this present life more than to God and his promises will lose it."

Another way to illuminate this paradox is to consider the context in which Jesus makes these claims. Jesus does not say, "Whoever hates his life will preserve it for eternal life," but rather, "Whoever hates his life *in this world* will preserve it for eternal life." (John 12:25) The hatred he upholds is hatred toward life *that* is less than eternal life—such as a life entirely immersed in things of the world. Likewise, Jesus does not say simply, "He who loses his life will find it" but rather, "He who loses his life *for my sake* will find it." (Mt. 10:39) In this context, Jesus focuses on the *intention* of the loss. The intention is to glorify God. A martyr may lose his life for the sake of bearing witness to a higher good or for the sake of saving someone else's life; but the martyr does not hate life in the sense that he does not recognize that it is good.

But what about hatred for one's family members? Why does Jesus seem to encourage us to hate our own family? How could such hatred be virtuous? Doesn't this contradict Jesus' command to love our brothers and sisters? Certainly, this is perplexing.

Here again, it is important to consider the context. In the passage just before the one in which Jesus mentions hating one's family members, he speaks of putting things before God and of using things —including relationships —as an excuse for delaying our "yes" to God. One may provide the excuse: "I have married a wife, and therefore cannot [follow God]" or, "I have bought a field, and I must go out and see it." (Lk 14:18 and 20) It is within this context that Jesus says, "If anyone comes to me without hating his father and mother, wife and children, brothers and sisters, and even his own life, he cannot be my disciple." (Lk 14:25) So Jesus is not proposing that we hate our family in the sense that we should not have charity toward them or in the sense that we fail to see them as gifts from God, but only in the sense that we do not put them before God and use them as an excuse to delay our commitment to God.

Something similar comes to light when we consider the context of Jesus' words about bringing the sword and setting family members against each other. (Mt 10:34-36) Following this passage, Jesus says, "He who loves father or mother more than me is not worthy of me; and he who loves son or daughter more than me is not worthy of me." (Mt 10:37) Again, he is not proposing that we ought to hate our family or seek discord with them but that we should love God first and foremost. Nowhere does he say we should be devoid of charity towards our family. But he does warn us that if we put God first, people might reject us or bear hostility toward us. Following Jesus is not a thorn-less rose garden.

Paradox of The Cross and Resurrection

One of the most striking of all Christological paradoxes is that of the cross and resurrection. Many see it not just as perplexing or contradictory, but as a scandal. (cf: 1 Corinthians 1:23) He who says he is "the life" suffers, dies on a cross, and descends into hell. This simply is not supposed to happen!

To add to this perplexity, we are told that Christ is without sin and yet he is not only condemned as a criminal but condemned for our sake. "For our sake he made him to be sin who did not know sin, so that we might become the

righteousness of God in him." (2 Cor 5:21) It seems prepos-
terously unjust that an innocent man should die for the
guilty.

The first step in illuminating this paradox is to
acknowledge that it goes way beyond what we can comprehend through reason alone. No amount of reasoning without the aid of faith will bring us to the conclusion that life is
commensurate with death and that the innocent should be
crucified. To approach this paradox with the illusion that
reason can resolve the paradox entirely is to set oneself up
for disappointment. This does not mean however that reason cannot be of help. The cross is one of the most difficult
of paradoxes to illuminate, but it can be done insofar as it
can be shown that it is not contradictory to say that Jesus is
"the life" and also that Jesus "died the most ignominious
death."

St. John Paul II acknowledges that "the preaching of
Christ crucified and risen is the reef upon which the link between faith and philosophy can break up." (*Fides et Ratio,*
23) By doing so, he affirms that it is impossible for reason
alone to comprehend such a mystery and that it will always
remain a mystery. Nevertheless, he also asserts that Christ
crucified and risen "is the reef beyond which [faith and phi-
losophy] can set forth upon the boundless ocean of truth."
(Ibid.) Reason takes us far, but it can only answer some questions. To find answers to other questions (such as, "Is there
an afterlife?" and "What is the ultimate meaning of life?"),

reason must rely on faith. Reason takes us to the edge of the cliff where land and water meet, then faith must join with reason to continue the journey.

The second step in illuminating this is to look to the person and teaching of Jesus. Pondering his attitude toward death and his passion and resurrection can help reason answer questions about the possibility of an afterlife.

Jesus' own resurrection is foreshadowed in his interaction with the girl who was thought to be dead but was only sleeping and in the raising of Lazarus. By raising others from the dead, and by himself rising from the dead, he gives us reason to hope for life beyond death. Many scoffed at Jesus when he said the girl is not dead but merely sleeping. They feared that he was being insensitive to the father of the child and setting him up for disappointment. Likewise, many though it was impossible for Lazarus to be risen and that it was foolish even to go near his decaying, stinking body. Reason says, "No way! It's not possible. So don't even try." But Jesus gives reason an extra wing and thereby provides us with hope as we begin the journey into the supra-rational and super-natural.

By Jesus' own resurrection, he gives us even more reason to believe and hope in an afterlife. He proclaimed that he *would* resurrect and then he showed us that he is a man of his word, not a delusional idealist. Had he not risen, there would be reason to doubt all his promises, but by fulfilling this promise to rise, he gives us a reason to trust that what seems to be impossible is actually possible.[6]

Had Jesus not risen, it would be difficult if not impossible to illuminate the paradox of his passion and death. St. Paul reminds us, "if Christ has not been raised, then our preaching is in vain and your faith is in vain. If Christ has not been raised, your faith is futile and you are still in your sins." (1 Cor 15: 13-14) Had he died and not risen, there would be no easy and coherent way of answering the questions, "Why did he go willingly to this crucifixion and death? Why did he not save himself?" But in the context of his resurrection, these questions can be answered. He went willingly (and not suicidally) to his death because he *knew* he would rise, he *knew* he would give his followers reason to hope for life eternal, and he *knew* he would be bearing witness to selfless love and thereby providing us with an example to imitate. He did not expect us to believe the absurd, namely, that he who is "the life" is dead. Rather, he gave us a reason to believe that

---

[6] The fact that the disciples were willing to be martyred for proclaiming that Jesus rose is also significant. If they did not witness the resurrection and have reason to believe that it really occurred, we would be at a loss for explaining why they were willing to die. For a fuller treatment of evidence for the resurrection, see *The Son Rises: Historical Evidence for the Resurrection of Jesus*, William Lane Craig)

although it is paradoxical that he died, it is not absurd to believe that he is indeed "the life."

The resurrection illuminates the passion and death but also the Incarnation. Only in the light of the resurrection does the Incarnation make sense. Why did God become incarnate? To show us that he is with us, that he has not abandoned us, that he loves us with pure and unselfish love, and that he is merciful. Why should we believe that he is indeed who he said he was? Because he fulfilled promises that he would not have been able to fulfill if he wasn't.

The Incarnation and resurrection of Jesus also provide us with a perfect example of compassion. He becomes one of us, enters into our condition, and shields himself not from suffering, precisely because he felt empathy and was willing to suffer with his people, to console them, to heal them, to feed them, to cleanse them, to enter into their poverty, to live amongst them, and to even suffer with them.

This is the primary and best example of compassion and shows very clearly that empathy bears fruit. Evil had hold of the world and Christ entered into it—and even into hell—in order to bring love. Those who wish to imitate him must be willing to do as he did. They must have the courage to suffer with others. But this is not suffering for the sake of suffering; it is suffering for the sake of the fruit of suffering, that is, for the sake of love. Love conquers evil.

So, although the Cross and death of Jesus may seem to be a contradiction, absurdity, and scandal, it is possible for us to make sense of them if we consider it in the broader context of the fruit of the Cross. In spite of initial appearances, the Cross is the source of life, hope, and compassion. It is an icon of God's love, not a logical absurdity.

THE "WORD OF GOD" AND THE PARADOX OF INEFFABILITY

Why do we call Jesus "The Word of God" if God is beyond words?

In the Prologue of the Gospel of St. John, Jesus is called the *Logos,* which is usually translated as *The Word.* What is a word?

A word entails communication. It is through a word that that which was previously unknown or hidden becomes known. A word likewise entails revelation. Jesus is the *Word* in the sense that he reveals God to us, thereby making him better known to us.

Though words are normally spoken or written, in the case of the *Logos* this is not an essential component. God can communicate with us and reveal himself to us in ways that often transcend mere writing and speaking. Likewise, though words are normally distinct from both the person speaking and the concept to which the word refers, *The Word* is not distinct in this way.

The paradox then is this: God is ineffable (that is, beyond words) but Jesus is the "Word." It is certainly odd, and seemingly contradictory, that the ineffable would be given the title "Word." It would seem that "No Word" would be a better title and that it would be even better if Jesus was not given a title at all. In short, we are left with the question: Why do we call that which is beyond words "the Word".

The paradox of the "Word" is part of the paradox of the Incarnation. To illuminate one is to illuminate the other. It is not a contradiction to say that Jesus is God, that God is ineffable, or that Jesus is the Word, provided we understand what it means to say that God is ineffable. He is not ineffable in the sense that absolutely nothing can be said about him, nor in the sense that he is not capable of communicating with us, but only in the sense that we cannot fully know him (even if we know him in every way that we possibly can through faith and reason). Never could words suffice to explain the heights and depths of his being and his love.

Thus, Jesus is not the *Logos* in that he reveals everything to us, but in the sense that he reveals aspects of God which we cannot know through reason alone to us. The Logos is, as it were, a prism through which the divine light is refracted so we can appreciate the intricacies of God and his love for us; yet he is more than just the prism, he is also the light.

Jesus is able to reveal God to us in ways that go beyond what we can know of him through reason alone, and he is also able to reveal God to us in a profoundly human way, that is, in a way which is in accord with our nature. We are sensate beings; and it is in and through Jesus we can come to know God in a way that is sensate. Like St. Thomas the Apostle, we can look and feel that God is with us, and this can be of particular consolation when we are tempted to doubt his existence or his love for us. We are also communal; and it is in and through Jesus we can encounter God in a communal way. He comes to us as one of us—born into a family and a society in which life consists of nitty gritty details. We are likewise intellective; and it is in and through Jesus' words to us that we can come to understand things we would not otherwise be able to understand. In short, through Jesus, God meets us where we are and in accord with our nature. Through the Incarnation, God speaks to us in our own language. The ineffability gap is bridged in the person of Christ.

There are many examples of how Jesus is able to bridge this gap. Let us look at some of the most striking of them. First, Jesus is able to show us *who* God is. As Aquinas asserts, through reason alone we can know *that* God exists, but we cannot know *what* or *who* he is. We can know through reason, that God is a first mover, a first cause, a necessary being upon which all else relies for its existence, a cause of goodness and other perfections, and the telos of all created things. (*ST* I, 2,3) But we cannot know anything else. It is Jesus who shows us that God is a being who is personal, loving, and Trinitarian. He shows us that God is a "who" not just a "what".

Moreover, Jesus shows us not only that God is loving and personal, but also that God is love and what love is. This is done in many ways, but the most striking is through his crucifixion. By dying for us, and letting blood and water flow from his side, he shows us that God loves us unconditionally, selflessly, infinitely, and in spite of our sinfulness. When St. Catherine asked why Jesus allowed his side to be lanced after he died, he responded, "There were plenty of reasons but I shall tell you one of the chief. My longing for humankind was infinite but the actual deed of bearing pain and torment was finite and could never show all the love I had. …I wanted you to see my inmost heart, so that you would see that I loved you more than finite suffering could show."[7] By dying for us, Jesus shows us that his love for us is "stronger than death." By rising, he shows us that there is reason to hope that there is more to life than just this present one. By sharing his Eucharist with us, he shows us that he is with us always. By crying to his Father "My God, my God, why have you abandoned me?" he shows us that we are not alone in our pain and that, though God may seem to be far away, he is with us. Philosophy does not teach us that God is love; Jesus does.

Through his living example, the Word shows us who we are supposed to be and how we are called to live. Reason can give us pointers on how to live. The pre-Christian philosophers wrote many magnificent treatises on the ethical life

---

[7] *The Dialogue*, section 75.

and provided insights into the nature of virtue which in turn provided a foundation for moral theology. Through natural law, we can grasp the good and the precept that "good is to be done and pursued and evil is to be avoided." Similarly, we can arguably grasp through reason alone that the following are goods: preservation of life, procreation and education of offspring, living peacefully in society, and seeking to know the truth. And from this we can derive precepts such as: we ought to preserve life, we ought to educate our offspring, we ought to live peacefully with others. (*ST* I-II, 94, 2) Nevertheless, through reason and philosophy alone, we cannot know precepts related to our supernatural call and our supernatural end. We cannot know, for example, that we are called to love God with all our heart, soul, and mind (Mt. 22:37); nor can we know that we are called to love our enemies. It is through the Word, and his living example, that we come to know the intricacies of how we are to live. He shows us, through example, what perfect, selfless love is and that we are called to the same kind of love.

Through his preaching, the Word again bridges the gap. He shows us, for example, that we are called to be friends with God. Though Aristotle provided us with great insight into the importance and nature of friendship, he was not able to discover that friendship with God is possible and that we are called to such friendship. Reason alone enabled him to see the importance of the question of whether we can be friends with God; however, without revelation and the

Incarnation, Aristotle was left thinking that there is too much inequality between God and man for there to be true friendship between them.[8] It is only through the Word that this came to be known. The Word himself, through his teaching tells us, "You are my friends." (Mt. 15:14)

Through his Sacraments, the Word again bridges the gap. He shows us that he remains with us, even after his resurrection, by providing us with healing, continued forgiveness, and the grace to continue growing in his love. And most importantly, he gives us the Eucharist, "in which the ... unity between the signifier an the signified makes it possible to grasp the depths of the mystery." (*Fides et Ratio,* 13) In the Eucharist, as in his Incarnation, he is the "Word made flesh."

Through his relationship with his Father, the Word again bridges the gap by showing us who the Father is. He claims to be one with the Father, to reveal the name of the Father to us, to hand on the word of the Father to us, to be in the Father as the Father is in him, and to have been sent by the Father (Jn 10:30-38; 17:21-23; 17:6-8). He also claims that he came into the world to bring us to perfection, to union with the Father, and to a deeper understanding of the Father's love. (Jn 17:21-23; 26) In short, he bridges the gap (and is the Word) by giving us a glimpse of the Father which we otherwise would not have. When we see Christ, we see

---

[8] See Aristotle, *Nicomachean Ethics* Book VIII.

the Father. (Jn 12:44-45) And so Christ is the Word specifically in the sense that he is the word of the Father.

In short, Jesus is the Word in the sense that he shows us what we cannot know through reason alone. We have the words and logic of the philosophers, but they only get us so far. We need the Word, the *Logos*, to take us the rest of the way. There is a logic in this. God loves us and gives us the ability to know that he exists using reason alone; but precisely because he loves us infinitely, he also gives us the ability to know him more profoundly through the Incarnation. He made us in such a way that we have a thirst to know and love him in a way that transcends the natural. For this reason, he gave us—through the Word—a supernatural knowledge of him and the supernatural grace necessary to love him with the theological virtue of charity.

PARADOXES OF CELIBACY AND VIRGINITY

There are many paradoxes of celibacy. It is barren, but fruitful; abstemious, but passionate; seemingly contrary to natural law and perhaps impossible, yet not; and angelic, but human. It is no wonder that so many look askance at celibacy and hold it suspect. How could someone think that the God who commanded us to "be fruitful and multiply" call some people to be celibate? How is it even possible to be celibate? Isn't it unnatural and unhealthy to be celibate? Why would God want such a thing? The many difficulties inherent in resolving these paradoxes and questions has led many to doubt Mary's perpetual virginity, the celibacy of Christ, and the prudence of priestly celibacy and the consecrated life. Let us look at these paradoxes in greater detail.

First, celibacy is paradoxical in that it is barren and yet can be immensely fruitful. Indeed, it is often the case that, "the barren wife bears seven sons but the mother of many languishes." (I Sam 1-10) Mary is the example *par excellence* of this. She is a virgin yet a mother; and not just any mother, but the mother of Christ, the mother of the Church, and the "New Eve." Virgin martyrs are also a good example. Though they bear no children and even sometimes give up their lives on account of their fidelity to their vows, they are the "seed of the Church" and have inspired many to follow Christ more intimately. Mother Teresa is yet another good example. Celibate though she was, she was a mother to thousands and thousands of orphans. It is not by accident that superiors of women's communities are frequently called "Mother." So, though it is paradoxical that celibacy can bear great fruit, when looked at through a spiritual lens, it makes perfect sense.

Second, celibacy is paradoxical in that it is abstemious yet passionate. The idea of abstention, fasting, penance, and asceticism usually conjures up the image of passionless stoics. Passion and abstention seem to be mutually exclusive. Yet in the writings of many virgin saints, one finds great passion. The *Song of Songs,* an erotic love poem, is often seen by such mystics as the best allegory of the spiritual life. Therein we read such phrases as:

> Let him kiss me with kisses of his mouth, for your love is better than wine. (*Song of Songs*, 1:1)

> The King has brought me to his bed chambers. (1:4)

> You have ravished my heart, my sister, my bride; you have ravished my heart with one glance of your eyes, with one bead of your necklace. (4:9)

> I belong to my lover, and my lover belongs to me.... (6:3)

Though these passages are replete with passion, they are lauded by many mystics and virgin Saints as being great metaphors of the spiritual life. St. Teresa, St. John of the Cross, St. Bernard of Clairvaux, St. Catherine of Siena, and others frequently echo them in their own works. Though the life of the celibate has elements of the acetic, it can be the most romantic and passionate of all lives. It is the writings and example of these Saints that illuminate this paradox.

Third, celibacy is paradoxical in that it seems to be contrary to nature and therefore also unlawful. Just as it would be against nature and natural law to abstain from all food, so, too, it would seem to be against nature and natural law to

abstain from all sexual intercourse. (*ST* II-II, 152, 2) Moreover, since we are called to "increase and multiply," it would
also seem to be against Divine Law. (Gen 2:16)

To illuminate this paradox, let us turn to Aquinas. From
a natural law perspective, he shows that virginity is lawful if
lived out in the context of society. Provided that there are
some people who bear fruit in a biological sense, it is not necessary for each individual to do so. (*ST* II-II,152,2, obj. 1)
Preserving the human race and keeping it in existence is necessary, but it is obviously possible to do so without everyone
procreating. It would even make sense to say that it can be
beneficial to society for some people to forgo having children
provided that those who do so help foster the well-being of
others in some way. Think, for example, of the fruit born by
Sisters who have apostolates in teaching, nursing, and ministry to the poorest of the poor. Think of the thousands upon
thousands of people who have been cared for by the Mission-
aries of Charity. One need not have children to play a role in
preserving and bettering human life.

Aquinas also points out that virginity is lawful if it is undertaken for the right motive. Were one to choose a life of
perpetual virginity simply for the sake of oneself (perhaps to
avoid being bothered by children or to pursue one's own
dreams of luxury and success, with no concern for the well-
being of others) such a choice would not be praiseworthy.
Were one to choose a life of virginity out of disdain for the
body (heretical or otherwise) or extreme prudishness, such a

choice would likewise not be praiseworthy. When, on the other hand, one chooses a life of virginity for the sake of a higher purpose (such as contemplation of the divine and loving service to others) one's choice is good. Not only is it lawful and in accord with Divine Law, but it is also even praiseworthy.

A fifth paradox is that celibacy would seem to be impossible. Just as it would be impossible for someone to abstain from all food and water (at least not without there being serious ramifications), so, too, it would seem to be impossible to be perpetually celibate. It is often argued that the Catholic Church is unwise to expect priests and consecrated persons to take vows of celibacy. Oddly enough, the vow of celibacy is even frequently blamed for the lack of fidelity of those who have taken such vows—as if not making a vow of celibacy will prevent lust and perversion.

This paradox of the supposed impossibility of authentic celibacy can only be adequately illuminated by looking at it as a gift and a grace. Given our fallen nature, without grace, praiseworthy celibacy—undertaken within the context of society and with the right motive—is indeed impossible. With grace, however, all things are possible. It is for this reason that it is essential to discern whether the grace of celibacy has indeed been given to an individual before one takes such a vow. Not all can live a vow of celibacy, "but only those to whom that is granted." (Matthew 19: 11) To attempt to live such a life well is futile without grace.

Finally, celibacy is paradoxical in that it is angelic—when lived well—and yet profoundly human. In the early Church, those who practiced asceticism and embraced perpetual virginity were compared to the angels and said to imitate the angelic life. For example, St. Basil states, "men and women who keep virginity are angels, and not of a common kind, but of a very high and noble class."[9] Similarly, St. John of Damascus states, "celibacy is… an imitation of the angels. For that reason, virginity is as much more honorable than marriage, as the angel is higher than a human being."[10] How is it possible for humans (who are bodily by nature) to imitate angels (who are non-bodily by nature)? It would seem that by choosing the life of angels, humans would cease to be human and possibly even fall into an unhealthy, vicious, and heretical angelism.

The key to illuminating this paradox is to consider the *way* in which a celibate person imitates the life of the angels. Angels, being incorporeal, are within the realm of the intelligible. They are free from the cares of the flesh and so are free look upon the face of God without distraction. The celibate person imitates the life of the angels insofar as he is

---

[9]https://en.wikisource.org/wiki/States_of_Christian_Life_and_Vocation,_According_to_the_Doctors_and_Theologians_of_the_Church/Part_1/Section_1/Article_2/Paragraph_2._Virginity/Chapter_2

[10] St. John of Damascus, *Exposition of the Christian Faith*, 4.24.

(ideally) freer from the cares of the flesh than he otherwise would be. Nevertheless, the celibate does not cease to be human in the sense that he becomes incorporeal. He remains embodied and maintains all the facets entailed therein, including the duty to perform corporal works of mercy when they are necessary. If a celibate were to act as the Pharisee in the parable of the Good Samaritan, he would incur guilt.

So, celibacy is not contrary to human nature, nor does it entail becoming incorporeal. It is natural but also supernatural. Supernatural grace, including the grace of perpetual celibacy, "does not destroy the natural, but elevates and perfects it." (*ST* I, 1, 8, ad. 2) Moreover, given the fact that God has created us not only with a natural end but also with a supernatural one, it follows that celibacy *for the sake of the Kingdom* is profoundly human.

THE PARADOX OF THE BEATITUDES

Not all of the beatitudes spoken of in the Sermon on the Mount are paradoxical, but many of them are. It is not terribly puzzling that the clean of heart will see God (Mt 5:8), that the peacemakers will be called children of God, (Mt 5:9) or that the merciful will be shone mercy (Mt 5:7). It should be the clean of heart who see the spotless Lamb; and it is the peacemakers—those who serve the God of peace—who should be called children of God. It should likewise be the merciful who are shown mercy, and it is no great surprise that those who are merciful with others are in turn shown mercy.

Though some of the beatitudes are not paradoxical, others are. Let us look at them in more detail.

"Blessed are the poor in spirit, for theirs is the kingdom of heaven." (Mt 5:3)

This is paradoxical at best, contradictory at worst. How can one who is poor be blessed? This would seem less paradoxical if Jesus said, "theirs *will be* the kingdom of heaven," but he says, "theirs *is* the kingdom of heaven." How is it possible for the poor to have even the smallest of earthly kingdoms, much less the kingdom of heaven?

This paradox can be illuminated by considering two words: *spirit* and *heaven*. The Lord is not speaking of just any poverty, he is speaking of poverty of spirit. Similarly, it is not speaking of just any kingdom, he is speaking about the kingdom of heaven. The one who is poor in spirit is the one who does not cling to temporary, passing things which moths can destroy. (Mt 6:20) It is rather the one who does cling to such things who is poor, since such a one is enslaved to an insatiable thirst. The more we have, the more we want. Having a luxury watch does not quench the desire to possess; it increases it. The luxury watch can lead to the desire for a luxury car; the luxury car can lead to the desire for a luxury home; the luxury home can lead to the desire for luxury vacations. It can become a vicious and insatiable circle.

The one who is poor in spirit is also the one who has given himself away to the other and hence has found himself and his highest purpose —his *raison d'etre*. As St. John Paul II so eloquently put it, "Man… cannot fully find himself except through a sincere gift of himself." (*Gaudium et spes* 24) Those who are poor in spirit are not simply those who do not possess earthly luxuries, but they are also those who do not possess *themselves* and have thereby found true fulfilment through self-transcendent love. They are the ones who experience true ecstasy by going out of themselves.

The kingdom which the poor in spirit inherit is the kingdom of *heaven*—the beatific vision. By nature, we are not merely corporeal. Even those who have all their corporeal needs met still have other needs, such as the need for friendship and a sense of purpose. Even pagan philosophers can recognize this. The kingdom of heaven is the only kingdom that satiates because it is the only kingdom which quells all our longings. Our higher needs, not just corporeal needs, are met only when our hearts and minds have what they were made for: God. The poor in Spirit are those who are not strapped down by material belongings, and it is they who are free to soar into God and into his kingdom.

"Blessed are they who mourn, for they will be comforted." (Mt 5:4)

This is indeed perplexing. Those who mourn seldom if ever think they are blessed. Thus, the word to emphasize here is *will*. Those who mourn *will* be comforted. This beatitude is gives us reason to hope insofar as it is a promise for future comfort and a promise for an afterlife. If there was no possibility of seeing our departed loved ones in the future, there would be no reason for Our Lord to use the word *will* in, "will be comforted."

Another important point here is that it is only those who have loved who mourn. Nobody mourns the loss of someone they have not loved. So, although those who mourn experience sorrow, they can at least be comforted by knowing that they have loved and have had the opportunity to enjoy the gift of friendship. This comfort can be amplified by looking at it in the context of the life to come, but it is a comfort in this present life as well. Blessed are those who mourn, for they have loved, do love, and will continue to love another person.

"Blessed are the meek, for they will inherit the land."
(Mt 5:5)

This too is perplexing—though perhaps not as perplexing as some of the other beatitudes. It is not difficult to imagine a meek person as a land-owner; but it is nevertheless odd that Jesus tells us that it is *specifically* the meek who will inherit the land.

So, what is it to be meek? And what kind of land are we talking about anyway? To be meek is to be humble, gentle, and receptive. The opposite is to be proud, disgruntled, greedy, and to think that we possess what we have because we have acquired it by our own efforts. An inheritance is something that is received, not earned, and receiving something unearned can be humbling (not humiliating, hopefully, but humbling). As was pointed out earlier, to be humble is to be close to the earth. So, it is the meek who can inherit the land. It is they who are already close to the land, and it is they who are receptive. It is no surprise then that it is also they who are in the best position to inherit the land.

The land Jesus refers to is land that "will be" inherited. He does not promise us great things now, but he does give us a promissory note for the future. Elsewhere, he reminds us to be attentive. He compares the kingdom of heaven to vigilant virgins who are ready when the Bridegroom arrives. (Mt 25:1-13) He also reminds us that it is the faithful and prudent servant, who does not fall into foolishness while the master is away, who will be put in charge of all his master's property. (Mt 24:45-47) Looking at his promise within this context, it is clear that he is calling us to be habitually meek as we wait for our inheritance.

In short, the land to which Jesus refers is eschatological land. What the meek will inherit is not land that can be bought and sold—given and taken—in this life, but land that will endure. Like the living water offered by Jesus to the woman at the well, this type of land will not leave us wanting more—it will leave us content and hence truly blessed.

"Blessed are they who hunger and thirst for right-eousness, for they will be satisfied." (Mt 5:6)

It is difficult to trust that righteousness will prevail. The world we live in is full of corruption, sin, violence, exploitation of the weak, and everything that is contrary to righteousness. But this paradoxical beatitude gives us reason to hope. Those who hunger and thirst for righteousness *will* be satisfied—in spite of all present appearances.

In this beatitude, it is not just any hunger and thirst that Jesus promises to satisfy; it is specifically hunger and thirst for righteousness. Jesus does not promise that all types of longings will be satisfied, but he does promise that the longing for righteousness will be. This is a hope-filled message for our world in which only unrighteousness seems to prevail. Day after day, year after year, century after century, the corrupt seem to triumph. With the psalmist, we cry out:

How long, LORD, shall the wicked,
how long shall the wicked glory?
How long will they mouth haughty speeches,
go on boasting, all these evildoers?
They crush your people, LORD,
torment your very own.

They kill the widow and alien;

the orphan they murder.

They say, 'The LORD does not see;

the God of Jacob takes no notice.' (Ps 94)

This beatitude is Jesus' response to the psalmist. It is his way of saying, "do not be dismayed by the unjust. They will not forever triumph. Do not give up. Persevere in righteousness."

The paradox of this beatitude is at the heart of all paradoxes of faith insofar as all paradoxes of faith require just that—faith. Through illumination of paradoxes, we can come to see that it is not irrational to have faith and hope. Faith and hope in the Word of God and his message can inoculate us against cynicism and despair. Blessed are we who are given the beatitudes. The beatitudes themselves are a light in the darkness.

"Blessed are they who are persecuted for the sake of righteousness, for theirs is the kingdom of heaven." (Mt 5:10)

This is truly odd. Who in their right mind would feel blessed for being persecuted? Who in their right mind would rejoice when being calumniated? (Mt 5:10-11) This beatitude only takes on light when we look at the next phrase: "rejoice and be glad, for your reward will be great in heaven.

Thus, they persecuted the prophets who were before you. (Mt 5:12)

St. Francis understood this beatitude well. He told his little confrere, Br. Leo, that true joy is not found in receiving praise, working great miracles, being learned, converting souls, or even raising the dead; rather, it is found in suffering with Christ. He describes such suffering as entailing rejection, homelessness, hunger, insults, and mockery. The picture he paints of perfect joy is at first glance dismal indeed. The highest of all graces, St. Francis maintains, is "the grace of overcoming oneself, and accepting willingly, out of love for Christ, all suffering, injury, discomfort, and contempt."[11]

It is difficult indeed to make sense of this. How can one rejoice when being insulted? How can one rejoice when suffering? Let us look at two ways of illuminating this.

The first way is to note that this beatitude, like some of the others, is eschatological in nature. It is a promise for what is to come, not for a cessation of the evil that is present. Jesus illuminates this by telling us that our reward in heaven *will* be great. It is a beatitude of hope; and hope is easy to rejoice in.

The second way is to recognize it as a sign that one is indeed following the Lord. Being insulted and persecuted may seem to be a curse, but when we consider that Christ as well as many of his true followers were insulted and persecuted,

---

[11] *Little Flowers of St. Francis,* Chapter VIII.

it is possible to see it as a blessing. Our Lord promises us that "if they persecute me, they will also persecute you." Likewise, he promises us that if we belong to him and not to the world, the world will hate us. (Jn 15:18-20) So, provided we are not suffering on account of our own sins or ill behavior, we can rejoice, knowing that we are being treated as he was.

THE PARADOX
OF ACTION AND CONTEMPLATION

Saying that works of mercy and prayer are two necessary aspects of the spiritual life is common, but the nuances of the relation between them frequently get ignored. Many people focus on action and think that too much prayer is unnecessary and perhaps even a waste of time given that we live in a world in which there is so much need. These people have a point. We are, after all, encouraged not to "babble on like the pagans, who think that they will be heard because of their many words." (Mt 6:7) Others focus on contemplation and think action is unnecessary if one is living an authentic life of prayer. These people, too, have a point. After all, many demons can only be cast out through prayer, and it is Mary, not Martha, who chose the one thing necessary. (Mark 9:29; Luke10:42)

The paradox is this: those who criticize the purely contemplative life, such as the life of the Carthusians and hermits, are sometimes told that they understand neither the

Catholic tradition nor what the contemplative life really is. On the other hand, those who criticize the active life are sometimes accused of Pelagianism and a failure to rely on God's grace and providence.

Before delving more into this, a word on terminology is in order. The *vita activa*, the active life, entails outward expressions of love for one's neighbor such as corporal and spiritual works of mercy including feeding the hungry, giving drink to the thirsty, sheltering the homeless, visiting the sick, visiting prisoners, burying the dead, giving alms to the poor, counseling the doubtful, instructing the ignorant, admonishing the sinner, comforting the sorrowful, forgiving injuries, and bearing wrongs patiently. The *vita contemplativa*, the contemplative life, entails praying for the living and the dead (which is a spiritual work of mercy, and which does not require direct interaction with one's brothers and sisters), as well as spending time in meditation of truth (including study, discursive meditation, mystical non-discursive prayer, prayer of quiet, petition, adoration, thanksgiving, prayer, and praise).

An example of someone who lives a purely active life would be a Christian Peace Corps volunteer or missionary who has no prayer life. An example of someone who lives a purely contemplative life would be a recluse or hermit who has a life of prayer but lives in complete solitude and has no direct human contact.

Objections to the purely contemplative life:

One objection to the purely contemplative life is that a life devoid of any works of mercy would be antithetical to living the commands of the Gospel. Christ gives many, many admonitions regarding exterior, active charity. These can be clearly seen in the Parable of the Good Samaritan (Lk 10:25-37) and in the Judgment of the Nations (Mt 25:31-46). In these passages, Christ indicates that the *vita activa* is a necessary condition for salvation. Love of God and neighbor are both necessary to inherit eternal life, and Jesus specifies that love of neighbor requires showing mercy to others. Those who pass by the needy and victimized—even though they may be on their way to pray in the temple—are identified as those who do not have love for neighbor. (Lk 10:25-37) Similarly, those who do not respond to the needs of the hungry, thirsty, naked, ill, strangers, and imprisoned will be those to whom the Son of Man says "depart from me you evil doers into the eternal fire prepared for the devil and all his angels." (Mt 25:31-46)

James provides us with an equally strong admonition. "If a brother or sister has nothing to wear and has no food for the day, and one of you says to them, 'Go in peace, keep warm, and eat well,' but you do not give them the necessities of the body, what good is it? So also faith of itself, if it does not have works, is dead. … a person is justified by works and not by faith alone." (2:14-17; 24)

Another objection to the purely contemplative life is that it does not seem to provide opportunities to grow in charity and could in principle be lived by someone without any charity whatsoever. It is indeed unclear how living in complete solitude could lead to self-transcendence and loving the other for the sake of the other. Even though one could argue that the hermit can live purely for the sake of God, this could easily be dismissed as disingenuous; after all, God does not need our prayers. It seems that if someone wanted to do something for the sake of God, the best thing he could do would be to love his brothers and sisters, in whom Jesus dwells.

In *The Dialogue,* God the Father shows St. Catherine that he *could* have made us each self-sufficient but that he intentionally made it necessary for us to rely on each other precisely so that we can grow in charity.[12] To this it could be added that if God wanted us to live purely contemplative lives, he would have made us angels, not humans. Angels, being incorporeal, are never in corporeal need; and, since they do not exist in time, they do not need people to pray for them. They need neither spiritual nor corporal works of mercy to survive. We do.

A hermit might be asked, "How do you justify your life of complete contemplation in light of the above passages and in light of the fact that there are so many people who are in

---

[12] Catherine of Siena, *The Dialogue*, section 7.

dire need?" Numerous inadequate responses to these objections could be given. Let us look at a few and show why they are inadequate.

(1) **Hermit's Response:** "I am preparing for the beatific vision and so I do not need to respond to my brothers and sisters who are in need."

Critique of the Hermit: The problem here is obvious: according to many Scriptural passages, there will be no beatific vision if we neglect those in need.

(2) **Hermit Response:** "I have entered into solitude in order to work out my salvation and grow in holiness."

Critique: The problem here is that working out one's salvation and growing in holiness, if done in an authentic way, requires following Jesus' command to love—which in turn requires responding to the needs of others.

(3) **Hermit:** "I am living the life of the angels."

Critique: The problem with this response is that if God wanted this poor hermit to be an angel, he would have created him as one.

(4) **Hermit:** "I did not know Jesus wanted me to respond to the needs of others."

Critique: The problem here is that only if one does not read Scripture can he be ignorant of such things and, moreover, it is a very central tenet of the Gospel. So, this response would only fly if the poor hermit was indeed ignorant through no fault of his own.

(5) **Hermit:** "I am called to the purely contemplative life. It is that simple. Not everybody has the same vocation."

Critique: Although one may be called to be a hermit, he is not thereby exempt from charity. Even hermits are called to charity. If a starving person were to show up at the door of a hermit, and this hermit intentionally did nothing, he would fail in regard to the greatest of the commandments.

(6) **Hermit:** "I was afraid I might fall into pride if I responded to the needs of others. After all, someone might see me and praise me."

Critique: Although we are indeed called to be humble in the sight of God, and not blow trumpets before our works of mercy, it does not follow that we should not engage in such works. Yes, pride might seep in, but "love cancels a multitude of sins." Love can make up for a lack of humility, but humility cannot make up for a lack of love. The greatest of all the virtues is love (not humility, nor faith, nor hope). Moreover, Jesus admonishes us to use our talents and not bury them out of fear.

(7) **Hermit:** "My heart is burning with love for God and others, that is enough."

Critique: This is a lovely response, but it would lead to challenging and rather rude rhetorical questions such as: "How can you say you are 'burning with love' if you are not doing unto others what you would want them to do unto you? If you were a destitute mother with seven starving children, would you really want all those who could help (including hermits) to do nothing?" So, the problem here is that only if the hermit indeed would not want help if he were a destitute mother would his response bear weight.

(8) **Hermit:** "I am focused on 'the one thing necessary' as Mary was. I'm sure God would not want it to be taken from me."

Critique: Although Jesus indeed told Martha that Mary's contemplation was 'the one thing necessary,' he did not say it was necessary *and* sufficient, nor did he say that Mary was forever off the hook in terms of responding to the needs of her brothers and sisters.

(9) **Hermit:** "Jesus spent time in the desert, praying and fasting. I am imitating him."

Critique: Although Jesus spent time in the desert, he also spent time in public ministry, preaching, healing, casting out demons, and other such things. To fully imitate him, one must be active and contemplative—both.

The problem with the purely active life:

It is very difficult to justify the purely contemplative life, devoid of all external works of mercy, but it is likewise very difficult to justify the purely active life, devoid of all prayer. Before attempting to help our hermit find a satisfactory response, let us look at some of the problems with the purely active life. This time, let us ask a missionary who lives a purely active life the following question: "Why, in light of the Gospel message, do you live a purely active life?" Let us also critique his responses.

(1) **Missionary's Response:** "I live a purely active life because in the Gospel Jesus calls us to works of mercy. Life is short and *now* is the time to act. In the hereafter, when people are no longer in need, I will have the opportunity to live the *vita contemplativa* (provided I go to heaven, of course)."

Critique of the Missionary: This is a good response insofar as the missionary clearly acknowledges Christ's call to works of mercy. Nevertheless, it is problematic insofar as it presupposes—rather than establishes—that prayer and the contemplative life are incompatible with a life given to works of mercy.

(2) **Missionary:** "When I pray, all I can hear is the cry of the poor. Just as a mother cannot sit and pray while her baby is crying, I cannot sit and pray while people are in need."

Critique: This, too, is a good response. It shows that the missionary is very mindful of the needs of the poor. However, like the previous response, it presupposes that prayer and action are incompatible. (It also sounds as if the missionary is a bit scrupulous.)

(3) **Missionary:** "We are all called to be different parts of the mystical body and imitate Jesus in different ways. Some are called to imitate him in the desert by living the *vita contemplativa*. However, I am called to imitate him in his public ministry and service of others. I am his hands."

Critique: Our missionary has a point here. Not everybody is called to be the same part of the mystical body. However, it does not follow that just because someone is called to be the hands, he is not also called to be the heart (which is the contemplative life). Without being united to the heart in some way, a hand will quickly rot.

(4) **Missionary:** "Jesus says that whatsoever we do to others, we do to him. I love him and cannot sit on my chair of contemplation knowing that I am neglecting him. If Jesus is really in the poor, and if I am really striving to be his disciple, I cannot turn a blind eye to them. To neglect the poor is to neglect Jesus."

Critique: Once again, the missionary has given a nice response. Jesus indeed tells us what we do for others we do for him, and what we fail to do for others we fail to do for him. However, the problem is that, although Jesus indeed tells us this, he does not tell us that we do not need to pray. The missionary has fallen into a *non sequitur.*

The Illumination

One of the reasons there can be confusion about the distinction between the *vita contemplativa* and *vita activa* is that it is easy to look at the distinction between these two in temporal and spatial ways. It is easy to think that to live an authentically contemplative life, one must spend lots of time in prayer and solitude. However, in reality, the contemplative life can transcend these limitations. One can pray anytime and anywhere.

We see a glimpse of this reality in the Parable of the Pharisee and the Tax Collector. (Lk 18:9-14) The Pharisee spent plenty of time praying, but his prayer was not authentic. It was merely a litany of self-congratulatory egotism. And although the tax collector's prayer was quite short, his prayer was quite authentic. All he said was, "Oh God, be merciful to me a sinner." Again, we see this reality in Jesus' response when he is asked by his followers how to pray. He warns against "babbling on," and he thereby shows that prayer need not be lengthy to be authentic. (Mt 6:7). Thus, to live an authentic life of prayer, to live the contemplative life, one need not be a hermit.

Another reason why there is confusion about the distinction between the two ways of life is that there is too much emphasis on the differences between them. The two ways are different, but they are by no means mutually exclusive, nor should they be. The contemplative life can be lived authentically only if it incorporates elements of the active life; and vice versa. St. Therese, a missionary in a cloister, who wanted to "spend her heaven doing good on earth," is a good example of this; so, too, are St. Francis, St. Catherine of Siena, St. Dominic, St. Thomas Aquinas, and so many others. They were all profoundly active and profoundly contemplative. And Jesus is of course the example *par excellence* of this. At times he was a desert-dweller, and at times he was a city-boy.

One of the Dominican mottos is: *Contemplare et contemplata aliis tradere,* which can be translated as, 'to contemplate and to share with others the fruits of contemplation.' This motto creates a beautiful bridge between the two lives. In contemplation, one can receive from God that which he needs in order to live the active life effectively. "It is in giving that we receive." (Prayer of St. Francis) It is also in receiving—from God through prayer—that we have something to give.

In light of this, let us return to our hermit and missionary. A satisfactory answer that the hermit could give would be, "I live in solitude, but I pray daily for the living and the dead (which is a spiritual work of mercy), and I likewise pray for those living the apostolic life. I am not here just for myself, but also for others; and if a destitute mother and her children where to knock on my door, I would immediately put on my apron and serve them to the best of my ability."

A satisfactory answer the missionary could give would be: "I see Christ in the poor and I adore him in them. I live the active life, I engage in works of mercy, but my heart keeps vigil within me, and so I also live the contemplative life." The response of the hermit reveals that his life is not devoid of charity and works of mercy even though he is hidden. He is not in the desert to navel-gaze. And the response of the missionary reveals that his life is not devoid of contemplation. Both of them are living the "both/and" vocation to which Jesus calls all his followers.

In the words of Raissa Maritain, "if contemplation ceases entirely, hearts would be dried up.... Love of one's neighbor, as well as love of God, obliges the contemplative to remain close to the divine source."[13] Without the *vita contemplativa*, the *vita activa* will sooner or later die. However, without the *vita activa*, the *vita contemplativa* will cease to be authentic. The two are necessary in the mystical body of Christ as a whole as well as in each individual person. No follower of Christ is exempt from either.

---

[13] Jacques Maritain, *Peasant of the Garrone* (Oregon: WIPF and STOCK, 1968), 223. Jacques is quoting Raissa Maritain, *Journal de Raissa*, op. cit., p.67.)

PART III

PHILOSOPHICAL PARADOXES

PARODOXES OF REASON

Paradoxes of reason are legion and is precisely for this reason that philosophy is perennial. Since the dawn of civilization, there have been peripatetics of all sorts wandering in search of knowledge and wisdom. From the ancient Greeks to the modern, bohemian hipsters, there have always been questioning souls—people looking for answers. As a full exploration of paradoxes of reason would take an eternity, and as we do not have an eternity to take, we will look only at a few. They will include paradoxes regarding the knowledge of God, the paradox of speaking about God who is ineffable, existential paradoxes, and the information paradox. We will also look at scientism and show that, though it may seem to be merely paradoxical, it is actually contradictory.

Exploring these paradoxes will entail looking at the following questions: If God is so far above us, how can we possibly know anything about him? If God is ineffable, why do we attempt to speak about him? Doesn't law limit our freedom? Isn't "being" boring? Is Socrates right to say that the unexamined life is not worth living? Does access to information make us wise? And, finally, is scientism scientific?

PARADOX OF THE KNOWLEDGE OF GOD

The overall gist of this paradox is that God is God and we are not, and yet we are (supposedly) able to know him and (supposedly) supposed to seek him. In the Book of Isaiah, we read, "For my thoughts are not your thoughts, neither are your ways my ways, says the Lord. For as the heavens are higher than the earth, so are my ways higher than your ways and my thought than your thoughts." (Isaiah 55: 8-9) Yet, we also read, "Seek the Lord while he may be found, call upon him while he is near...." (Isaiah 55:6) And we also read, "Be still and know that I am God." (Ps. 46:10) How is it possible to know God if he is so far beyond us? How is it possible to seek that which cannot know? Why would God ask us to do the impossible?

We are in a fine mess now! God is everywhere and nowhere. God is to be sought, but he cannot be found. To illuminate this, let us look at what some of the Saints teach us regarding the nature of knowledge and some of the ways in which we can know God.

The nature of knowledge:

Aquinas teaches that when we know something, we know it according to our own mode or nature (and not the mode or nature of the thing known). He states, "a thing known exists in a knower according to the mode of the knower." (*Quidquid reciptur ad modum reipientis recipitur.*) (ST I, 14,1, ad 3.) What does this mean?

In this scenario, we are the knowers, God is the known. We are finite, sentient, and intellective creatures, so we know in a finite, sentient, and intellective way. The difficulty here is that God is beyond us. He is infinite, and it is for this reason that we cannot know him as he is in himself. It is also for this reason that The Psalmist says, "To me, how mysterious your thoughts, the sum of them not to be numbered! If I count them, they are more than the sand; to finish, I must be eternal, like you." (Ps 139)

To further illustrate this, imagine looking at the sun through rose-colored lenses. In this scenario, the light of the sun will always appear as rose-colored, even though the sun itself is not. The light will, in a sense, appear to the viewer in the mode of the lenses because it is filtered through them. Analogously, knowledge of God is not knowledge of God exactly as he is in himself but knowledge of him from our limited perspective. When we see light through colored lenses, we know it not as it is in itself but as it is after it gets filtered through the lens; and when we know God, we know him not as he is in himself but as he is after he gets "filtered" through our finite minds.

The many ways to knowledge of God:

There are many approaches to coming to knowledge of God. Many of these ways are abstract and philosophical. Others are intuitive and personal. When it comes to approaches to knowledge of God, there are perhaps as many ways as there are people who seek and find God. After all, we know God according to our own mode and no two believers are the same. The egg-headed philosophers seek and sometimes find him through reason, logic, and deductive reasoning. Others—perhaps the majority of believers—find him by some other route. Witnessing the birth of a child may bring one person to knowledge of God; reasoning about the cause of motion may bring another to such knowledge. Let us look at a small sample of some of these ways, beginning with the more abstract and proceeding to the more intuitive, and then return to our paradox.

Abstract Ways

Ontological Ways

Some have come to knowledge of the existence of God through reason alone. Such knowledge is rarely a dramatic or dynamic type of knowledge, nor one which is frequently life-altering in the way a personal conversion experience might be, but it is a type of knowledge, nevertheless.

Numerous philosophers, including St. Anselm and Descartes, have attempted to provide proofs for the existence of God using deductive arguments that utilize the definition of God or the concept of God as starting points. For readers who are not familiar with such arguments, let us take a quick look at Anselm's. Anselm states,

"Well then, Lord, You who give understanding to faith, grant me that I may understand ... that You exist as we believe You to exist, and that You are what we believe You to be. Now we believe that You are something than which nothing greater can be thought. Or can it be that a thing of such a nature does not exist, since 'the Fool has said in his heart, there is no God' [Ps. 13.1; 52:1]? But surely, when this same Fool hears what I am speaking about, namely 'something-than-which-nothing-greater-can-be-thought', he understands what he hears, and what he understands is in his mind, even if he does not understand that it actually exists. For it is one thing for an object to exist in the mind, and another thing to understand that an object actually exists. Thus, when a painter plans beforehand what he is going to execute, he has [the picture] in his mind, but he does not yet think that it actually exists because he has not yet executed it. However, when he has actually painted it, then he both has it in his mind and understands that it exists because he has now made it. Even the Fool, then, is forced to agree that 'something-than-which-nothing-greater-can-be-thought' cannot exist in the mind, since he understands this when he hears it, and whatever is understood is in the mind. And surely that than-which-nothing-greater-can-be-thought cannot exist in the mind alone. For if it exists solely in the mind, it can be thought to exist in reality also, which is greater. If then that-than-which-

nothing-greater-can-be-thought cannot-be-thought exists in the mind alone, this same that-than-which-a-
greater-can-be-thought is that-than-which-a-greater-
can-be-thought. But this is obviously impossible. Therefore there is absolutely no doubt that something-than-
which-a-greater-cannot-be-thought exists in both in the
mind and in reality."[14]

There is much debate about how best to interpret Anselm and whether his proof is sound, but even if it is, it would
provide us only with an abstract knowledge of God. This
type of knowledge would be akin to knowledge of a mathematical proof—interesting to some, perhaps, but not so interesting to others.

Cosmological Ways

Another type of abstract knowledge of God comes from
empirically-based, cosmological arguments. These types of
arguments begin not with the definition or concept of God,
but with that which is observable. Aquinas's famous "Five
Ways," for example all start with the empirical. The first be-
gins with our observation of motion; the second, with our

---

[14] Anselm of Canterbury. *Proslogion, in Anselm of Canterbury:
The Major Works,* edited by B. Davies and G.R. Evans, transelated
by M.J. Charelsworth, 82-ff.

observation of causality; the third, with our observation that some things come into existence and pass out of existence; the fourth, with our observation that some things are more good, true, and noble than others; and fifth, with our observation that things act for an end and that many things happen always or for the most part or in a relatively predictable fashion. (*ST* I, 2, 3) [15]

---

[15] For readers who are not already familiar with these ways, here is a quick peek at the first way:

The first and more manifest way is the argument from motion. It is certain, and evident to our senses, that in the world some things are in motion. Now whatever is in motion is put in motion by another, for nothing can be in motion except it is in potentiality to that towards which it is in motion; whereas a thing moves inasmuch as it is in act. For motion is nothing else than the reduction of something from potentiality to actuality. But nothing can be reduced from potentiality to actuality, except by something in a state of actuality. Thus that which is actually hot, as fire, makes wood, which is potentially hot, to be actually hot, and thereby moves and changes it. Now it is not possible that the same thing should be at once in actuality and potentiality in the same respect, but only in different respects. For what is actually hot cannot simultaneously be potentially hot; but it is simultaneously potentially cold. It is therefore impossible that in the same respect and in the same way a thing should be both mover and

In this first way, as is the case with his others, Aquinas claims that there cannot be an infinite regress, otherwise there would be no explanation for what we observe. In this first way, there cannot be an infinite regress of moved movers because then we would not have an explanation for why there is motion at all. In other words, if everything that moves was itself put into motion, we would not be able to explain why there is motion. If A is in motion because it was put in motion by Z, and Z is in motion because it was put in motion by X, and X is in motion because it was put into motion by Y, we never have an explanation for why there is motion. Saying that "it is turtles all the way down" doesn't work. Even if we suppose a circular set of moved movers, it does not help us. All it does is leave us with questions such as, "Why is there any motion at all?" and "Why does the set of moved movers move?"

---

moved, i.e. that it should move itself. Therefore, whatever is in motion must be put in motion by another. If that by which it is put in motion be itself put in motion, then this also must needs be put in motion by another, and that by another again. But this cannot go on to infinity, because then there would be no first mover, and, consequently, no other mover; seeing that subsequent movers move only inasmuch as they are put in motion by the first mover; as the staff moves only because it is put in motion by the hand. Therefore it is necessary to arrive at a first mover, put in motion by no other; and this everyone understands to be God.

Upon making the claim that there cannot be an infinite regress, Aquinas then concludes with the existence of "God". In this first way God is the first mover. In the second, God is the first efficient cause; in the third, God is a necessary being which does not rely on anything else for its existence; in the fourth, God is the cause of cause of goodness and perfection in things; and, in the fifth, God is an intelligent being to which all things are directed as their end. Provided that these arguments are sound, they provide us with a knowledge of God which is abstract in nature. They do not enable us to know that God is loving, trinitarian, or personal, but they do enable us to know that a first mover, first efficient cause, necessary being, etc., exists.

The Way of Design

Can one know God through empirical science? It may seem odd, to some, that there can be a type of knowledge of God through science. Many scientists would shudder at the claim that one can know God through use of the scientific method given that there is no empirical observation that could even in principle be made which would verify or falsify the claim that God exists. Likewise, it is impossible even to imagine how we might devise an experiment which would enable us to test the God hypothesis.

These challenges notwithstanding, there are scientists who claim that science points to something beyond itself. New design theorists, for example, claim that there are phenomena (such as the highly sophisticated bacterial flagellum) that cannot be explained without positing the existence of a designer. The claim that such phenomena could have originated by chance, evolution, or some non-conscious mechanism, they say, is so far-fetched that it is worthy of dismissal.

Yet, even for those who are convinced of the existence of a designer, it is not clear that the designer must be a God in the traditional theistic sense. A designer could in principle be a non-divine, finite, mortal entity of some sort.

So, does this lead to a type of knowledge of God? That depends on what you mean by "God." If by "God," you mean "that which is the explanation for phenomena that cannot be explained via mere scientific laws," then yes. If by "God," you mean "an omniscient, omnipotent, eternal, creator of all that exists," then no. To be an amazing designer, it is not necessary to have these Godly qualities. In spite of limitations, this type of argument for the existence of a designer (or God in a limited sense) can leave us with a sense of awe and an awareness that not all things can be explained by mechanistic thinking. It can thereby pave the way for openness.

Intuitive Ways

The Aesthetic Way

Many people find God through the aesthetic: through art, poetry, music, beautiful fragrances, and nature. There are many examples in the *Song of Songs* and in the poetry of St. John of the Cross of knowledge of God through nature. It is not uncommon for people to experience the divine, or the divine likeness, in natural beauty. In *The Spiritual Canticle*,[16] St. John of the Cross lets the Bride, that is, the soul who seeks God, ask nature a question:

> *"Oh woods and thickets*
> *Planted by the hand of my Beloved!*
> *O green meadow,*
> *Coated, bright, with flowers,*
> *Tell me, has he passed by you?*

St. John then lets nature respond:

> *Pouring out a thousand graces*
> *He passed these groves in haste*

---

[16] St. John of the Cross, *The Spiritual Canticle*, stanzas 4-5 in *Collected Works of John of the Cross* (Washington D.C.: ICS Publishers, 2017), 74

And having looked at them,
With his image alone,
Clothed them in beauty."

Nature is not God, but nature is clothed in beauty by being looked upon by God. Beauty itself clothes nature with
beauty and thereby makes himself known via nature. It is not
a face-to-face knowledge, but it is a knowledge nevertheless.
It is like knowing the whereabouts of a flower by smelling its
fragrance. Follow beauty and you will come close to God
even though you might not meet with him face-to-face.

Personal Ways

Many people also come to know God through profound,
life-changing experiences such as the birth of a child, marriage, and deep conversions. For example, someone may ask
the rhetorical question, "How is it possible *not* to believe in
the existence of God when a new child is born?" This type of
experience is, for many, a window to knowledge of God. It is
by no means something everybody experiences, but it is not
an uncommon experience. It is one of many ways of knowing God.

Interpersonal Ways

Interpersonal relationships, or experiences of self-transcendence can be another route. St. John Paul II points out that "...belief is often humanly richer than mere evidence, because it involves an interpersonal relationship...." (*Fides et Ratio*, 32) One's own experiences can provide a type of knowledge of God, but experience of going out of oneself—through charity, sacrifice, or self-surrender—is another. As God is charity, it follows that living in charity leads, at least implicitly, to a connatural knowledge of God. "To love another person is to see the face of God." (*Les Misérables* musical)

The experience of self-transcendence which can emerge in friendship is likewise a type of knowledge (and ideally should exist within every marriage). It is a type of self-evident knowledge which transcends the type of knowledge attained through abstract reasoning. The lover cannot doubt that he is in love, when he is in love, any more than the conscious person can doubt that he is conscious when he is conscious. This type of knowledge echoes—but far surpasses—Descartes's "I think therefore I am." It replaces the "I think, therefore I am" with: "I love, therefore my beloved is, and I belong to him." (cf. *Song of Songs* 6:3) Paradoxically, the "I" becomes fully itself by surrendering itself to the other. In losing itself, it comes to know the other, and in knowing the other, it finds certitude of the existence of love.

The experience of ecstasy that many mystics report is a good example of knowledge of God through self-transcendence. The term, which originates from the Greek term *ekstasis*, can be translated as *standing outside oneself*. (*ek* means 'out' and *stasis* means 'stand') This is a type of self-transcendence that St. Paul describes when he says, "I know a man in Christ who... was caught up to the third heaven—whether in the body or out of the body I do not know. God knows." (2 Cor 12:2) To go beyond oneself is perhaps the most intense type of knowledge of God possible for humans.

The Way of Discursive Meditation

Discursive meditation, or discursive prayer, is another route. This can include praying the rosary and meditating on different aspects of the life of Christ. It can also include *lectio divina* or reflectively reading spiritual books. It may be accompanied with verbal prayer, but not necessarily. It may also be accompanied by reflecting on the relation between what one is meditating on and her own life. For example, one may consider the Sermon on the Mount, imagine that she is sitting in the presence of Christ, and then consider ways in which she might apply the principles in the Sermon to her own life. Meditation of this sort can bring one to a knowledge of God in a way having a discussion with a friend can bring one to knowledge of the friend.

Apparitions

There are many examples in the lives of the Saints of knowledge of God through apparitions. St. Margaret Mary's experience of the Sacred Heart of Jesus, St. Faustina's experience of the Divine Mercy, and St. Bernadette's experience of Our Lady of Lourdes are just a few. These experiences are akin to discursive knowledge of God insofar as they involve specific aspects of Christ (and Our Lady) and can have a verbal component. Often, apparitions are accompanied by verbal messages. St. Faustina, for example, was able to write voluminously the words of Christ. Likewise, St. Margaret Mary was able to state verbatim what Christ told her. These apparitions, in turn, have provided other people with material for *lectio divina* and meditation.

Mystical, Non-Discursive Ways

There are many different types of mystical experiences, and they can all provide one with knowledge of God. Mystical knowledge can overlap with aesthetic, personal, and interpersonal types. They are often mutually inclusive. Mystical knowledge of God is arguably the most dramatic of all forms, and it is not something one can attain by one's own efforts. It is a supernatural grace and can, in some cases, be accompanied by ecstasy, apparitions, and locutions. Let us look more closely at some of these.

Prayer of quiet is a type of mystical knowledge, and it can be described as a simple gazing upon God or "the other." Discursive prayer is akin to having a discussion; prayer of quiet is akin to two lovers gazing into each other's eyes and thereby speaking volumes without saying a single word. Prayer of quiet is non-discursive insofar as it does not entail considering one thing, and then another, and then another. It is a simple and quiet resting in the present moment. St. John Vianney asked one of his parishioners what he does when he sits in the presence of the Blessed Sacrament. The parishioner responded, "I look at him and he looks at me." This is the prayer of quiet: a quiet resting in the presence of God. The prayer of quiet provides a type of knowledge of God and can provide one with a sense of God's simplicity.

Knowledge of the Indwelling of God within one's own soul is another type of mystical knowledge. St. Augustine and St. Elizabeth of the Trinity speak of this type of experience. St. Elizabeth, a Carmelite nun and contemporary of St. Therese, is known for her Trinitarian spirituality involving attentiveness to the Indwelling of the Trinity within her. In asking for the grace to know God in this way, she says, "Help me to forget myself entirely that I may be established in You as still and as peaceful as if my soul were already in eternity." To this she adds, "give peace to my soul; make it Your heaven, Your beloved dwelling and Your resting place." What she is asking is to become a tabernacle in which God can rest.

Elsewhere she says, "This is how I understand [the phrase] *belong to the House of God*: it is in living in the bosom of the tranquil Trinity, in my interior abyss, in this *invincible fortress of holy recollection*."[17] She was aware that her name means 'house of God,' as her Mother Prioress had told her, and she felt that her vocation was to be attentive to the Indwelling within her soul, within her abyss.[18] Elizabeth spoke of her soul as an abyss and of God as an abyss, thereby suggesting that she experienced a sort of mutual indwelling. God lived in her and she lived in him. Her soul was an abyss in which the abyss of God dwelt. Two years before her death she petitioned God: "Bury Yourself in me that I may bury myself in you until I depart to contemplate in Your light the abyss of Your greatness."[19]

One thing that all mystical knowledge has in common is that the experience is not something the mystic is capable of describing using words. For example, St. Therese of Lisieux states, "How powerless I am to express in human language the secrets of heaven." Similarly, toward the end of his life, after having had a mystical experience, Aquinas stopped writing, telling his confrere, Reginald of Piperno, "I cannot

---

[17] Elizabeth of the Trinity, *Collected Works of Elizabeth of the Trinity*, Vol I (Washington D.C.: ICS Publishers, 1984), 162. Elizabeth is quoting St. John of the Cross.

[18] Ibid., 12.

[19] Ibid., 184.

[write] anymore. Everything I have written seems to me as straw in comparison with what I have seen."[20]

Intellectual Visions

St. Teresa also speaks of intellectual visions, another type of mystical knowledge, which she describes as an awareness of the presence of God. This awareness does not entail seeing anything interiorly or exteriorly. As such, it does not seem to be a knowledge of God that is based on our sentient nature. It is rather an intellectual awareness of the presence of God. She says, "It is like feeling someone near one in a dark place."[21] Though she says this experience is not based on sight, she says that it is clearer and more evident to the soul

---

[20] Jean-Pierre Torrell, *St. Thomas Aquinas*, Vol 1. Trans. Robert Royal (CUA Press: Washington, D.C. 2005). (My note: It is a straw man to claim that, since Aquinas said his work was straw, that his work is no good and we don't need to read his writings. *In comparison* to mystical knowledge, speculative and discursive knowledge is straw but only *in comparison*. Though a picture of the Grand Canyon is only a one-dimensional image—and hence cannot capture the depth and magnitude of the Canyon—a picture can provide a likeness. A lousy likeness, maybe, but a likeness, nevertheless.

[21] St. Teresa of Avila: *first letter to Father Rodrigo Alvarez.* Quoted by New Advent Catholic Encyclopedia article on "Apparitions and Visions."

than if it were. It is a type of knowledge which surpasses the sentient nature of the human person and seems to be based solely on the intellective nature.

Apophatic Knowledge

Numerous theologians have claimed that the only knowledge we can have of God is apophatic knowledge, namely, knowledge of what God is not. Such theologians claim that God is so unlike us that we are incapable of knowing what or who God is. They argue, for example, that's since we are finite, we cannot know the infinity of God; hence, saying that God is infinite is really just a way of saying that he is not finite. Likewise, since we are temporally limited, we do not know what eternity is; hence, saying that God is eternal is really just a way of saying that he is not temporally limited.[22]

Some mystics echo this apophatic way insofar as they speak of their experience of God as an "unknowing." St. Elizabeth of the Trinity, for example, frequently uses the term *nescivi,* which translates as "I no longer know anything."[23] To this, she adds, "I don't not want to know anything except 'to know Him.'"[24] She realizes that, as Christ taught Martha,

---

[22] Insert references to apophatic theologians.

[23] Elizabeth of the Trinity, *Last Retreat,* Days 1 and 2.

[24] Ibid. Elizabeth is quoting Phil 3:10

only one thing is necessary. It is not necessary to know things in the world or to attend to the stirrings of one's own consciousness. All that is necessary is to remain silent in the presence of God. In unknowing the things of the world, the soul comes to a knowing of God. This unknowing is knowing in the most profound way possible.

St. John of the Cross, too, speaks of an unknowing in his *Spiritual Canticle*:

> In the inner wine cellar
> I drank of my Beloved, and, when I went abroad
> Through all this valley
> I no longer knew anything
> And lost the herd which I was following. [25]

It is an *unknowing* in the sense that there is no longer an awareness of particular things. The meanderings of one's own mind, daydreams, awareness of images or forms, and all such things cease. (Stanza 26, 8 and 17) Is also an unknowing in the sense that the soul even loses a sense of oneself. Everything vanishes and is "dissolved in love" as the soul "passes out of the self to the Beloved." (Stanza 26,14)

This apophatic way makes sense. Even if one were to have knowledge of all things in the world, it would be pure ignorance in comparison to this "unknowledge." (Stanza 26,

---

[25] John of the Cross, *Spiritual Canticle*, Stanza 26.

13) It is, as it were, a quasi-knowledge of the simplicity of God. (Stanza 26,17) It is likened to a window being united with the light or a coal being united with the fire. (Stanza 26, 4) In a sense, the knower and the thing known become one. A paradox indeed!

How these Many Ways Illuminate the Paradox of the Knowledge of God

There are, of course, many other ways to knowledge of God. These are but a few. Having looked at this sample, we are now in a position to return to the paradox with which we started: God is God—infinite in nature and hence infinitely beyond us and our small minds—yet we are able to know him (in a sense) and to seek him.

Again, Aquinas claims that, "a thing known exists in a knower according to the mode of the knower." (ST I, 14,1, ad 3.) By nature, we are bodily, sensate, intellective, and spiritual. Because we are bodily and sensate, we can seek to come to knowledge of God through his physical creation. Because we are intellective, we can seek to come to knowledge of God through abstract reasoning, reflection, and meditation. Because we are made in the image and likeness of God and have the Trinity dwelling within us, we can seek to come to knowledge of God by turning inward. Because we are spiritual, we can come to knowledge of God by receiving this knowledge directly from him through supernatural grace.

Finally, because we are made for love, we can come to know God by loving. God is the hound of heaven who created us to know, love, and serve him. He knows our nature better than we do, and he has provided us with as many routes to him as we have facets.

THE PARADOX OF SPEAKING
ABOUT THE INEFFABLE

There are many reasons to suppose that we can speak about God. The most obvious is that we in point of fact *do* speak about God. Even to say, "we can say nothing of God," is to say something of God. In addition, preachers preach about God, theologians teach about God, Scripture is the Word of God, and Christ is the Word who spoke frequently about his Father.

However, there are also reasons to suppose that we cannot speak about God. First, Scripture says, "eye has not seen, and ear has not heard... what God has prepared for those who love him." (I Cor. 2:9) If even God's promised gifts to us are ineffable, how much more must he be? Second, even when we hear the word "God," it conjures up many different images. For some, it conjures up the image of a grey bearded man on a throne; for others, Vishnu; for others, a strict disciplinarian; for yet others, an image of Christ; for others, nothing at all; and for others, something else entirely. How can we possibly speak about something if we don't agree on what the word "God" even means? Third, we don't know God in his fullness, that is, we do not comprehend him. But to speak meaningfully about something, you have to know what you're talking about. To speak meaningfully about fig- mabodges, for example, we must know what they are. If we don't, we are simply out of luck. Likewise, to speak meaning- fully about God, it would seem that we must know *who*, *what*, or at least *that* he is. Finally, as noted above, toward the end of his life the Angelic Doctor himself said, "Every- thing I have written seems to me as straw in comparison with what I have seen."[26] If even Aquinas, with all his eloquence, admitted that what he said about God was mere straw, there is not much hope for the rest of us. So, the paradox here is that it seems we both can and cannot speak about God.

To illuminate this paradox, let us turn to Aquinas. Aqui- nas claims that "a thing is named by us according as we un- derstand it." (ST I, 13, 1, obj. 3) It follows from this that we can only speak about or name God insofar as we can know him or, in other words, it is only when we have an idea of God that we can connect that idea to a word. For example, it is only if we have an idea of God and goodness that we can meaningfully say, "God is good." If we know nothing of God or goodness, speaking of God's goodness is futile.

---

[26] Jean-Pierre Torrell, *St. Thomas Aquinas*, Vol 1. Trans. Rob- ert Royal (CUA Press: Washington, D.C. 2005), 298.

Given his teaching on how we name things—and given his teaching that we cannot know God perfectly—Aquinas claims that we cannot speak about him literally or perfectly. We know God via his effects, not directly, and so we speak of him accordingly. For example, if we know of God's existence by way of Aquinas's second way, we know God not as he is in himself but only indirectly as the first efficient cause. Likewise, if we know of God's love through a supernatural experience of him as an abyss (like St. Elizabeth of the Trinity did), we know him not as he is in himself but as he is in us (via his indwelling). Given that God is always far more than what we know of him, we cannot speak of him literally.

When we speak of God's attributes, we again cannot speak literally. In order to say meaningfully, "God is good," we need to have some idea not only of God but of goodness, but, as is the case with the existence of God, we only know of the goodness of God through his effects. More specifically, we know of God's goodness insofar as he is the cause of goodness in things. For this reason, when we say God is "good" and daisies are "good," we are not using the term "good" in the exact same way. (ST I, 13,5) When we say a daisy is "good," we do not mean it is goodness itself or the cause of goodness in other things; but when we say God is "good," we do mean he is goodness itself.

To make matters even more complicated, we come to define the term "good" by experiencing good things. For example, a child may come to know what the word "good" means by being shown a collection of good things such as daisies, music, art, people, sunsets, and puppies. These examples enable the child to abstract the concept of goodness. By seeing instances of good things, however, the child cannot come to comprehension of perfect, self-sustaining goodness which is the cause of the goodness in other things. She can come to a general concept of such a thing, but not to full comprehension. Thus, if she later calls God "good," she is using her limited concept of goodness and predicating it of God. No matter how nuanced her concept of goodness is, however, it will always be less than goodness itself, who is God.

Let us look at another example. When we say God is "wise" and Aquinas is "wise," we are not using the term "wise" in a univocal way. God's wisdom is not like our wisdom. When we say a person is "wise," we don't mean (ordinarily) that the person is wisdom itself. What we mean is that the person has the quality of being wise. Plato, for example, was wise insofar as he knew the limits of his knowledge. Aristotle was wise insofar as he was able to think critically about human action. Mother Teresa was wise insofar as she was compassionate. However, for all their wisdom, Plato, Aristotle, and Mother Teresa were not equivalent with wisdom itself. They were wise people, not wisdom.

This difference between God's wisdom and our creaturely wisdom is vast. When we say God is "wise," we mean (assuming we are being theologically correct) that he is wisdom itself. He is wise in the sense that he is all-knowing and this all-knowingness is identical to him. The same is true with God's love, omnipotence, and all his other attributes. When creatures are loving and powerful—regardless of how loving and powerful they are—they are not love and power itself. They merely have the quality of being loving and powerful; and, unlike God, their love and power are *distinct* qualities. In God, they are not distinct. God *is* by nature goodness, love, and power. His attributes are not separate from his being or nature.

Just as we do not speak about God univocally, we also do not speak about him equivocally, that is, in completely different ways. When we say, "God is good" and "flowers are good," we use the term "good" in a similar rather than entirely different way. On the contrary, when someone says, "he is a pitcher" and "he is drinking water out of a pitcher," the term "pitcher" is (hopefully) being used in two different ways. Since God's goodness is like the goodness of a flower— insofar as God is the cause of the goodness of the flower and insofar as the goodness of the flower is a reflection of God's goodness—we do not use the term "good" in an equivocal way. So, in short, we cannot speak about God or name him in either a univocal or equivocal way.

So, how *can* we speak about God? We can speak of him analogously. Put simply, we can speak of God in way that is similar but not identical to how we speak of creatures. When we say, "God knows," and "Aquinas knows," we mean something similar but not identical. God knows in the sense that he all-knowing; Aquinas knows in the sense that he knows many things but not everything. The same goes for many of the other things we say of God. When we say, "God is who is," we mean that he is being itself, the highest being, and the cause of being in everything else. However, when we say "Aquinas is," we mean that he receives his existence from God or—more technically—that he participates in God's existence. God's being and Aquinas's being are similar but not exactly the same.

So, though we cannot speak of God univocally or equivocally, we can speak of him analogously. The underlying rationale for this is that cause and effect have something but not everything in common. As God is the cause of creation, creation bears some resemblance to him. Although we do not know God directly, we know him indirectly through his effects. And since we form language via our knowledge of creation, it is possible to use language when speaking about God. Nevertheless, given the vast difference between God and creation, speaking about God will always be very far from perfect.

EXISTENTIAL PARADOXES

The term "existential" is used in oodles of ways, but it is typically used to refer to a branch of philosophy which focuses on the themes of being, existence, human freedom, angst, questions about the meaning of life (or lack of such meaning), and authenticity. Paradoxes about such themes are legion, and it could be said that paradox itself is one of the themes of existentialism. In any case, we will look here at paradoxes about existence itself, our attitude toward our existence, freedom, angst, and the meaning of life.

The Paradox of Existence

The fact that there is something rather than nothing is one of the greatest paradoxes of all and is certainly the most perduring. It is paradoxical insofar as existence is the most obvious fact and yet—in a sense—also the most mysterious. It is impossible *not* to know that there is something rather than nothing. As St. Augustine puts it, "If I am mistaken, I exist"; and as Descartes similarly puts it, "I think, therefore I am." I can doubt my own existence, but, in doubting it, it only becomes more evident that I exist. A doubting thing must exist in some way, of course, in order for it to doubt.

Although the fact that there is something rather than nothing is the most obvious of all facts, it is also the most mysterious insofar as it is impossible to fully explain. Even if I am the only thing that exists, I cannot explain *why* I exist. And if I am not the only thing that exists, I again cannot explain *why* that is so. It is perhaps precisely because it is impossible to fully explain that the mystery of existence is seldom acknowledged and—even when it is—it is frequently scoffed at. "There go those philosophers again, asking questions that can never be answered: 'How many angels fit on the head of a pin? Why is there something rather than nothing?' – Who knows and who cares? Get a life, philosophers and theologians!"

Although the mystery of existence is the thing that people tend to think about the least, it is in some ways the thing that people should think about the most. We are caught up with qualities, with accidentals, and with nonessentials. As Shelly Percy puts it, "the mist of familiarity obscures from us the wonder of our being." This is understandable and, in some ways, necessary. Nevertheless, we sometimes forget that without existence itself, there would be no accidental qualities; there would be no stop signs, places to go, things to do, dreams to catch, or people to watch. There would be nothing. The most wondrous thing is that there is anything at all.

Pondering the mystery of existence can be tremendously enlightening. Indeed, it can even bring one to a deeper knowledge of God and appreciation for all his works. Ponder a single lily. Qualitatively, it is brilliant, fragrant, and simple in its complexity. It has all these qualities and in itself it is marvelous. Yet even more extraordinary is the fact that it exists at all. It need not exist, nor its fragrance, nor its brilliance, nor any of its other qualities. How much richer our lives become when we ponder the simple profundity of being.

Raissa Maritain, wife of the great Jacques, experienced deeply the profundity of being. Describing it, she says, "It often happened that I experienced, through a sudden intuition, the reality of my being, of the profound, first principle which places me outside of nothingness. A powerful intuition, whose violence sometimes frightened me, and which has first given me the knowledge of a metaphysical absolute."[27] By the grace of God, she was able to see the magnificence of the fact that she *is*, that God's creation *is*, and that it has all been granted *ex nihilo*. We cannot merit a single ounce of existence; it is given gratuitously.

Sometimes, the profundity of existence goes unnoticed until the death of a loved one throws us into a stark realization of just how fragile and temporary our present life and circumstances can be. We are here today. This seems banal. This seems to be a given. But tomorrow all can be lost. How quickly things could change; how quickly I and all around me could cease. These thoughts can be dreary, when looked at from an atheistic perspective, but they can be profoundly transforming when looked at through the light of faith. "To be, or not to be? —That is the question." (*Hamlet*) How magnificent is being when its opposite is pondered.

---

[27] Raissa Maritain, *We Have Been Friends Together* (New York: Sheed and Ward, 1940).

The Paradox of Freedom

The term "free" is a loaded term. It is used to describe everything from the profane to the divine. There is free love, free loading, free lunch, free enterprise, Free Willy, free spiritedness, free will, and so on. The term can mean everything from freedom *from* (for example, "I am free from obligations") to freedom *to* (for example, "I am free *to* dedicate my life to you.")

There are oodles of paradoxes regarding freedom. The one we will focus on here is the paradox that true freedom requires wisdom, commitment, responsibility, discipline, and even foregoing options. High school students often cannot wait to move away from home so that they can finally be "free." Like birds, they long to be out of the cage so they can fly where they will. This is what I call "bird freedom." There are other types of freedom, however, that are more authentic. I call them quasi-freedom, sage-freedom, the freedom of the virtuous, and saint-freedom.

The higher and more authentic types of freedom paradoxically require an element of discipline or an element of what a bird or teen would consider a barrier to freedom. This is the paradox that is before us now. Let us look at these various types more closely.

Bird freedom is a freedom *from* anything that would hinder one from "doing what one wants." Hindrances to such freedom could include cages, cell walls, chains, prison guards, helicopter parents who like to ground their children, and thugs who make offers one cannot refuse. In short, bird freedom is freedom from restraint or compulsion.

Quasi freedom has bird freedom as a prerequisite. It includes freedom *from* restraint but also the ability to deliberate about possible means of attaining "what one wants." In the best of circumstances, birds have bird freedom, but they are not capable of having quasi freedom because they don't have the ability to deliberate about means to ends. And since they lack this, they frequently fail to attain what they think they want. The bird on the ground, joyfully and blithely eating seeds, can easily end up in the mouth of the cat.

Like quasi freedom, sage freedom requires having the ability to deliberate about ends and means to ends, but it also requires having the ability to distinguish between true goods and false or merely apparent goods. Someone with this type of freedom must have the wisdom necessary to discern what he *truly* wants and needs, as well as to identify things that may look appealing at first, but which have negative consequences in the end. As a result, the sage is able to discern between true happiness and apparent short-term thrills.

The freedom of the virtuous person entails all that sage freedom does but, in addition, the ability to do what it takes—in the real world—to attain that which he truly wants and needs. This is because the virtuous person has the ability to habitually choose the true good and to avoid that which is antithetical to it. He is consequently able to attain stable happiness and contentment. The virtuous person is freer than the others because he is the most adept at attaining the true good (even though, from the perspective of the bird or quasi-free person, he may seem to be enslaved or even caged by discipline.)

But we are getting ahead of ourselves. We have yet to explore the nature of authentic freedom and how it relates to authentic happiness, wants, and needs.

The term "happy" is ambiguous at best. One can be happy that the Bulls won, happy to see a loved-one, happy to be on a roller-coaster, happy to have something to eat, and so on. But there is a distinction between being happy in the sense of having a temporary emotional high (or what I call "roller-coaster happiness") and happy in the sense of being truly content and fulfilled. Aristotle's term *eudaimonia* captures the latter sense of happiness. *Eudaimonia* comes from the Greek words *eu* (which means good) and *daimon* (which means spirit). It has been translated as: well-being, flourishing, and "the state of having a good indwelling spirit."[28] Aristotle uses it to refer to authentic flourishing and human fulfillment that is long-lasting and semi-self-sufficient in the sense that it is not based on mere lucky circumstances.

What are needs? Authentic needs are those things that are necessary for sustenance such things as food, shelter, and safety. One who is starving, homeless, or in an unsafe war

---

[28] Britannica.com, see article on *Eudaimonia*.

zone is not likely to be in a state of *eudaimonia* (though he may be if he has saint freedom which we will return to later). Authentic needs, however, must be distinguished from false needs or needs which may *seem* to be necessary for happiness (from the perspective of the non-sage) but which are actually not. Examples of false needs include gourmet food, alcohol, luxuries, and other instantaneous but short-lived pleasures. Such false needs—though they may seem to be necessary for attaining *eudaimonia*—can in fact be antithetical to it insofar as they can have negative consequences or leave a person with an insatiable desire for more. A run-of-the-mill alcoholic may *think* he needs liquor to have *eudaimonia*, but liquor may very well be antithetical to it. Likewise, a glutton may think he needs vast amounts of gourmet food, but such would be antithetical to eudaimonia.

What are wants? *Authentic wants* are those things that are necessary and sufficient for attaining *eudaimonia*. Examples can include friendship and a sense of purpose—since they are both things that make life worth living. As Aristotle wisely remarked, "without friends nobody would choose to live, though he had all other goods; even rich men and those in possession of office and dominating power...." (*Nicomachean Ethics*, Book VIII) Authentic wants are distinct from mere apparent wants. Mere *apparent wants* can include, honor, status, wealth, and everything in the apparent needs category above; but such wants are *de facto* be antithetical to *eudaimonia*. A narcissist, for example, may think that he needs recognition and admiration in order to be fulfilled and, worse yet, he may spend much of his time attempting to gain recognition; but he does not in fact *need* recognition. Indeed, it could be the case that in attempting to gain recognition he may end up boasting, alienating others, and thereby being without authentic friendship which is necessary for *eudaimonia.*

How does this relate to freedom? Authentic freedom entails: (1) knowing what is in your true long-term best interest or, in other words, knowing what *eudaimonia* consists in, and therefore knowing what your *authentic wants and needs* are; (2) knowing the true means for attaining *eudaimonia*; and (3) having the ability to attain it and avoid pitfalls along the way. In short, authentic freedom is having both the knowledge and ability to attain *eudaimonia* and avoid that which is antithetical to it.

To illustrate this, consider several different scenarios. In the first, you have just been released from prison and left on the side of the highway, but you have no idea where to go and, even if you did, you do not have the means to attain it or even to deliberate about how to attain it.

In the second scenario, you have just been released from prison, but you have been taken to a home where you will be given the opportunity to pursue a career in business. You have always wanted to start your own doughnut shop, you have experience baking, it is something you greatly enjoy, and you have been given a loan to begin this next chapter in your life. In both scenarios, you have freedom *from* prison but only in the second scenario do you have freedom *to* pursue what is in your apparent good (which *may* coincidentally turn out to be your true good, though not necessarily). In the second scenario you are free in two ways; in the first, only in one.

Now let us consider a third scenario. You have been released from prison, taken to a home, and given a loan to begin your business; but you have also been given a savvy business consultant to help you get started. In this case, you are free in three ways: you are free *from* prison, you are free *to* pursue your dream, and you even have—thanks to your consultant—the ability to identify the best possible means to having a successful and hopefully *eudaimonistic* business. Nevertheless, in this case it turns out that you lack the energy to run your business and you have difficulty putting your consultant's suggestions into practice. Then, to make matters worse, you end up realizing you hate running your business. As a result, you begin regularly binging on doughnuts and eventually becoming confined to bed because of the ensuing health problems. At the end of the day, you are less free than the bird and the prisoner. At least birds are free to fly in their cages and prisoners are free to roam about in their cells.

In this third scenario, before your business starts to go downhill, you are freer than in the first or second scenarios, because you have wisdom (your savvy consultant) at your side. And, yet there is still something lacking, namely, the ability to put your wisdom into practice in a successful and long-lasting way.

Now consider the fourth scenario. This time you attain the freedom of the virtuous. You are released from prison, taken to a home, given a loan and your savvy consultant, and you also have the wherewithal to carry out your plan. Moreover, as you progress, you reach the point where you are able to run your business smoothly and successfully with little effort. You have all your authentic needs met and you attain your longed-for earthly *eudaimonia*. In this fourth scenario, you are truly free. You are free *from*, free *for*, able to identify your true good, and able to attain it. And, once you attain it, you are free in the sense you are finally content—at least in an earthly sense.

But what is necessary to attain the freedom of the virtuous? The answer: things such as commitment, responsibility, foregoing certain options, discipline, and courage (things which may *seem* from certain perspectives to be akin to cages). Commitment and responsibility are necessary because things don't happen overnight. To run a business, consistency and diligence are essential. (Payroll, quality-control, good customer relationships, cleanliness, and abiding by required codes—all are necessary.) Foregoing options is also necessary. To run a successful business, other options have to be passed up such as other career and life-style options. Nobody can do everything.

Here is a simpler example. A beginning art student may start out with a desire to "express herself." She may be eager to get out her supplies and try to capture what is in her heart. There would seem to be nothing standing in her way to paint with *any* color of paint, *any* stroke of the brush, *any* subject, and *any* style. The options seem to be wide open. She is like the bird who has been released from a cage and can fly in *any* direction. As she continues her study of art, she may feel that learning painting techniques and being given assignments with stipulations are a hindrance to her freedom of expression. Nevertheless, as she diligently masters the techniques, she will find that her options only increase. Whereas before, she did not know how to mix colors to get just the right shade, or how to use her brush to get just the right effect, now she does. And this is all thanks to her discipline and commitment.

Whether it is acknowledged or not, and whether it is desirable or not, there are *de facto* limits to what one can do without knowing the rules, tricks of the trade, and laws of nature. Though one might *feel* free even without knowing them, one is not truly free. It is only when one knows them and knows how to work within their parameters that one attains this true freedom.

This then is the paradox of true freedom: it can require commitment, responsibility, discipline, tedium, perseverance, and even foregoing certain other options. So, authentic freedom may not *seem* like freedom from the perspective of the bird; but it nevertheless does from the perspective of the sage and virtuous person.

The Paradox of Saint Freedom

It is within the context of this Paradox of Freedom that a paradox of faith, namely the paradox of Saint freedom, can be understood. Saint freedom includes not just the freedom to attain one's true earthly *eudaimonia*, but also to attain one's supernatural *eudaimonia*. The saint is the one who: (1) is wise and hence knows what the highest possible good is, namely, God and the beatific vision, (2) has the virtue necessary to pursue it, and (3) the grace necessary to attain it.

Regarding (1), the saint has not just natural knowledge of earthly good but also supernatural, faith-based, revealed knowledge of one's heavenly good. Regarding (2), the saint has not just the natural virtues of the virtuous person, but also the theological virtues of faith, hope, and charity. And, regarding (3), the saint has grace from on high, without which attainment of the beatific vision would be impossible.

What is paradoxical about saint freedom is that it does not require bird freedom. The saint can be imprisoned, chained, and even martyred but still be free. Moreover, saint freedom is the highest type of freedom. No one is as free as the saint.

Christ himself is, of course, the most perfect example of this type of freedom. Though he is the author of the universe, he chose to become imprisoned in the sense of being bound by all the limitations that come with having a human nature. He became a temporal, finite, earthly baby in swaddling clothes in a manger, in the middle of nowhere, surrounded by farm animals.

St. Maximillian Kolbe is also an extraordinary example of saint freedom. He was free but chose a path that led him to the prison cells of Auschwitz and ultimately to the grave. From the perspective of the virtuous pagan, this might seem like the antithesis of freedom, but from the perspective of the saint, this is the type of freedom that is worth dying for. Just as the quasi-free person might look at the freedom of the virtuous person and scoff, so, too, might the virtuous pagan look at the freedom of the saint and scoff.

Of course, reason alone cannot fathom this type of freedom. It is only within the context of knowing—through faith—that we have a supernatural end which transcends all earthly happiness, that this type of freedom is makes sense. The virtuous pagan is free in the sense that he attains earthly *eudaimonia,* but the saint is free in the sense that he, by grace, attains the beatific vision.

Aristotle claims that the highest type of *eudaimonia* possible is contemplation of the divine. He asserts that such contemplation involves using the highest of our faculties (the rational faculty) to ponder the highest possible object of reason (the divine). But he admits that such *eudaimonia* is only intermittent. The body, with its needs and temporal nature, must be tended to, regardless of how contemplative a person might be; and hence, earthly contemplation is never ceaseless. Had he known of the beatific vision and of God's grace, he would have been in awe of the possibilities. Through philosophy, he went far in discerning the true good and the path to it, but through no fault of his own he didn't see the half of it.

The freest of all free persons, then, is the one who attains what he *authentically* wants. The virtuous pagan finds freedom, yet he is bound in the sense that his *eudaimonia* is limited, intermittent, and leaves more to be desired. However, the saint finds type of freedom that is ultimately boundless, continual, and complete. Though the saint may be physically bound by walls and chains, and though he may even be burned alive, like Sts. Lawrence and Joan of Arc, his soul is freer than the bird's. The bird flies from his cage into the sky while the saint flies from earthly bonds into God.

The Paradox of Angst and the Meaning of Life

By nature, people are curious about life and the meaning of it. In his *Metaphysics*, Aristotle states, "all... by nature desire to know. An indication of this is the delight we take in our senses; for even apart from their usefulness they are loved for themselves; and above all others the sense of sight."[29] Another indication of this is that cultures—both ancient and modern, eastern and western—have a notion of the spiritual. Some cultures have highly sophisticated religions, with precepts, doctrines, elaborate rituals, and an answer to the question, "What is the meaning of life?" Other cultures have simple myths. And still other cultures—and subcultures—have an agnostic or even atheistic view of things. But what all cultures have in common is a curiosity about the meaning of life. Even those who claim that life has no meaning, and that there is no God or afterlife, have enough curiosity to ask questions about such things and formulate answers.

Socrates is known for his assertion that "the unexamined life is not worth living." The rational person does not, like a mere beast, live only in the moment without at least some perplexity. "Who am I? Where did I come from? Where am I going?" All of these are questions which—though difficult if not impossible to definitively answer—lurk about. Some are paralyzed with angst, not knowing what to do with their uncertainty. And some (those blasted existentialists) even recommend staring into this abyss.

The paradox here is that although the unexamined life may not be worth living, as Ralph McInerny once remarked, but "neither is the overexamined life." Some are so haunted

---

[29] Aristotle, *Metaphysics*, Book I.

by the abyss of uncertainty that they become paralyzed. Hamlet's "to be or not to be?" can become a curse.

Camus's best contribution to philosophy is arguably his insistence that we should ponder the question: why not just commit suicide? Those who really live, and who are paying attention, are those who are able to face the question honestly and look diligently for an answer. Many are not able. Many lack the courage. Many are not sane enough to embrace such "insanity."

Try it sometime. Ask an undergraduate why they do what they do. Ask them, "Why did you come to class today?" You will hear responses such as: "to get a degree," "to make a life for myself and my family," "to someday make more money than I would if I did not get a degree," "to placate my parents," and even "because I don't know what else to do right now." Then ask them, "Why do you want to make money?" You will hear "so I can live comfortably?" Then ask, "why do you want to live comfortably." Then you will hear who-knows-what. And if you keep pushing things, you will eventually hear something like, "I hate these questions!" or an honest "OMG!"

Humans are rational insofar as they do at least some things with a sense of purpose: "I'm going to the store to buy shoes" or "I'm building this house so I have a place to live." The problem, however, is that humans are often irrational insofar as they don't think about the *ultimate* purpose. The "why?" question is easy to answer until it pertains to the overall "why?"

And yet... and yet...

...trying *too* hard to answer the ultimate question can make it difficult or even impossible to find an answer. Angst can be a good thing, but it can also be fatal. It is sane to ask the "why?" question, but it is insane to dwell on it to such a degree that it brings one to despair.

It is by living in the present—and ceasing to ask the question repeatedly—that the answer can be found. To ask is part of life, and a necessary part, but to live in the present is also. Hence, paradoxically, finding the meaning of life requires not spending exorbitant amounts of time asking about its meaning. A balance is necessary.

SCIENTISM— PARADOX OR CONTRADICTION?

Scientism is one of the most common of all current ideologies, and it is one that puts a wedge between faith and reason. In this section, we will look at what it is and why, though it may appear to be a mere paradox, it is actually contradictory. This will help illustrate the importance of distinguishing between paradoxes and contradictions. Just as seeming contradictions can turn out to be mere paradoxes, so, too, can seeming paradoxes turn out to be contradictions.

There are numerous types of scientism but the one we will look at here is epistemic scientism.[30] Epistemic scientism embraces the claim that *science and science alone can bring us to knowledge*. More specifically, it embraces the claim that *the scientific method and the scientific method alone can bring us to knowledge*. The problem with this is that the scientific method cannot establish that scientism is true. Put differently, the scientific method is incompetent to prove that the scientific method is the only—or even the best—method for attaining knowledge.

Of course, the only way to test a theory using the scientific method is to devise a test that can be carried out empirically. For example, an astronomer could make the following hypothesis:

the celestial body Io is a planet.

Then he could devise a way to test this empirically. He could reason thus:

if Io Is a planet, it will not be seen orbiting another planet.

---

[30] For a list of different aspects of scientism, see Susan Haack, "Six Signs of Scientism," *LOGOS & EPISTEME,* III, 1 (2012): 75-95.

Then, if he observes Io circling a planet, he will be able to conclude that Io is not a planet.

But how can the theory that *the scientific method alone, can bring us to knowledge* be tested using the scientific method? What kind of observation could disprove the theory? What test could be devised to test the theory? The problem here is that there is none.

At this point, the proponent of scientism might hold that his claim is self-evident and that it does not need to be tested. He might reason that just as the claim that 5+5=10 does not need to be tested in order to know it is true, neither does the claim that the scientific method alone can bring us to knowledge. But this would be awkward. It would amount to asserting the following two claims:

(1) *I know that the scientific method alone can bring us to knowledge.*

(2) *I know this, because it is self-evident (not because it has been proven via the scientific method).*

So, the proponent of scientism at this point would have two options. He could deny the first claim, or he could deny the second claim. If he denies the first claim, however, he will no longer be a proponent of scientism. If he denies the second claim, he will be in the awkward position of having to say that he knows something but that he does not know it via the scientific method, in which case he would be contradicting himself. He would be like a singer singing, "I am not singing." This is not a logical contradiction since he would not be claiming that it is both true and false that the scientific method alone can bring us to knowledge. Nevertheless, it would be a performative contradiction. Neither the singer nor the proponent of scientism should be taken seriously; and not just because they are hypocrites, but because they are denying their claim by the way in which they claim it. It is not like the smoker saying, "People shouldn't smoke." Such a hypocrite is not denying his claim by smoking; he is merely showing that he does not live up to his own standards. The singing person and the proponent of scientism, however, are saying something and saying it in such a way that they are denying it.

What this shows us is that it is important to distinguish between a contradiction and a mere paradox. Paradoxes can be resolved insofar as they can be shown not to be contradictory. Paradoxes should be embraced. Contradictions, however, should be jettisoned lest they become intellectually cancerous.

PART IV

PARADOXES OF GOOD AND EVIL

PARADOX OF
THE PROBLEM OF SUFFERING

One of the most obvious and stark paradoxes within the context of traditional theism is the problem of suffering. Traditional theists claim that God is good, all-powerful, and all-knowing. The problem is that there is suffering in the world. It would seem that if God is good, he would not allow suffering to exist. Likewise, it would seem that if he is all-knowing, he would certainly know about the suffering. Finally, it would seem that if he is all-powerful, he certainly would do something to stop the suffering or, better yet, not allow it to occur in the first place. Being good, all-powerful, and all-knowing do not seem to jive.

There are many ways to solve this problem. As it is a perennial problem, philosophers and theologians have been chipping away at it for centuries. A full consideration of all these could easily fill thousands of pages, thus we will look only at several of the most common ones.

One of the simplest (and unfortunately most common) solutions is to deny the existence of God. If there is no God, the problem dissolves. God is off the hook because he does not exist. There are many atheists who have adopted this solution (often without exploring other solutions). Likewise, many who begin as believers come to be unbelievers when they are confronted with this problem in a personal way. It is easy, if one has not confronted much evil, to fail to see the relevance of the problem. When one has experienced grave evil in a personal way, however, it can be impossible *not* to see its relevance. How many people have lost their faith after losing a child or loved one? How many have lost their faith after a grave natural disaster?

A second possible solution to the problem is to hold that God does not know about the suffering. If God is not all-knowing, one can claim that—although God exists, is good, and is all powerful—he has not prevented suffering because he does not know about it. If he doesn't know about it, he is off the hook. A parent who through no fault of his own does not know his child is suffering is not necessarily a bad parent.

A third solution is to hold that God is not all-powerful. If God is not all-powerful, he again is off the hook. Why is there suffering in the world even though God does not will it? Because he *can't* do anything about it, but he would if he could. A parent who wills the best for his child cannot be blamed when his child is suffering *if* it is the case that he can't do anything to stop the suffering.

A fourth solution is to hold that God is not good or benevolent. If God is apathetic and indifferent to suffering, this explains why—in spite of the fact that he exists, is all-knowing, and all powerful—there is suffering in the world. Indeed, it is often the case that children suffer because of the indifference and irresponsibility of their parents. This solution claims that God is like a neglectful parent who *could* stop evil and *knows* about it, but simply doesn't care.

The problem with all of these solutions is that they reject the God of mainline Christianity, namely a God who exists, is omnipotent, omniscient, and benevolent. If God does not have these qualities, he does not fit the Christian description of "God". Therefore, those who wish to rationally uphold the existence of the traditional Christian God must at least establish that there is no contradiction entailed. Let us look at two methods for doing this.

Method One

The first method for doing this is to show that there is a distinction between *allowing* suffering and *willing* it, and that allowing suffering does not entail lack of benevolence. More specifically, this method involves showing that God *allows* suffering but does not *will* it, and that he only *allows* it because he knows that there is some greater good which comes from it — a good that outweighs the evil which comes from allowing it.

Utilizing this method requires looking honestly at the following questions and providing coherent responses to them:

(1) What is the difference between willing and allowing?

(2) Are there goods that can only be attained when evil is allowed? If so, do such goods outweigh the evil which is allowed?

(3) If God allows evil, what might his motive be or, in other words, is it possible that God could have a benevolent motive for allowing evil?

(4) Is it possible that the good of love outweighs the evil of evil-doing and evil-willing?

(5) If God is all powerful, why does he not find some other means to bring about the good of love?

(6) If there is no other means to bring about the good of love, doesn't it follow that God is not all powerful?

Responses:

(1) What is the difference between willing and allowing?

There is a difference between willing and allowing ,and it is possible to allow suffering without willing it. If a father *wills* his son to suffer for no other reason than to suffer, he is clearly not benevolent, he is malevolent. However, if the father *allows* his son to suffer but does not *will* it—and if he allows it because it is the *only* means to a good which outweighs the evil of suffering—he can rightly be said to be benevolent.[31] It is not a contradiction to say that someone is benevolent and that he allows suffering for a good reason.

> (2) Are there goods that can only be attained if evil is allowed and that outweigh the evil which is allowed?

There are many examples of goods that can only be attained if evil is allowed. A mother, for example, might will her child to live but find that the only way to preserve the child's life is to amputate his leg. In this case, the good (the life of the child) outweighs the evil (the child's leg being amputated). In our less-than-perfect world, there are many such examples.

> (3) If God allows evil, what might his motive be or, in other words, is it possible that God could have a benevolent motive for allowing evil?

It is possible that God could have a good motive for allowing evil. In order to adequately respond to this question, however, it is first necessary to consider the nature of love. Love, to be authentic, must be free. Love cannot be coerced. Consider two different scenarios. In the first, a man brings flowers home to his wife (a seemingly loving act), and his

---

[31] The literal meaning of benevolent is to will the good. In Latin, *bene* means good and *volent* means willing.

wife then asks him what motivated him to be so loving. Imagine then that he responds by saying, "I brought them because a thug promised to kill me if I didn't. But believe me, I wouldn't have brought them otherwise!" In this case the wife would not be impressed, nor would she feel loved. Why? Because in this scenario the husband was not fully free. Imagine, in a second scenario, that the husband responds: "Honey, I brought them, not because I had to, but simply because I want you to know how much I love you and how special you are to me." Assuming he is not lying, and assuming he does not have any ulterior motives, it would be right to conclude that his act was an act of love. Only when an act is free is it possible for it to be loving.

Here is another example. Imagine that Sonar, a non-conscious robot, goes out to the street with a bag of food in "her" hands. Let's also imagine that a starving boy then takes the food and eats it. Would this be a loving act on the part of Sonar? Assuming that she is not a conscious being and is not capable of having motives, the act would not be loving in any ordinary sense of the term. Good would come from the situation but it would not be the result of the robot's love. Why? Because the robot is not free. Non-conscious beings are not free, and so we neither blame them nor praise them. We may blame or praise the creator of the robot, assuming the creator himself is free, but we do not blame the robot.

Love must be free in order to be authentic, but freedom comes with hazards. If one is free, he can authentically love;

but if one is free, he can also authentically hate or authentically be indifferent. Freedom is a requisite for true love but when we misuse our freedom, we can bring about evil. It is quite possible that God allows us to sin but only because he wills for us to be free to love. In the case of the boy who needs to have his leg amputated, the mother is not evil even though she allows the amputation *precisely because* it is necessary to save the boy's life. She wills the good and only tolerates the evil. If God allows evil *precisely because* he wills that we have the freedom to love, he (like the mother) is not evil. He may tolerate our misuse of freedom while willing that we not misuse it, that is, he may tolerate evil while willing love.

Given our limited knowledge, it is impossible to know whether the world would be better (a) with no freedom, no love, no evil-doing, and hence no suffering, or, (b) with freedom and love but also with suffering. To establish that world (a) is better would require knowing with certainty that the absence of suffering outweighs the good of authentic and free love. But, precisely because this type of certainty is not possible, we are not justified if we conclude that it is irrational to hold that a benevolent, all-knowing, and all-powerful God exists. It is quite possible that God both exists and is benevolent even though he permits suffering. Only an all-knowing being would be capable of knowing which world is better.

Stated differently, it is possible to *imagine* that the world would be better if there was no suffering and no love, but simply being able to *imagine* that this world would be better does not prove that it would in fact be better. Analogously, it is possible to *imagine* a ten-mile-high skyscraper, but this does not prove that such a skyscraper is in fact possible to build. Being able to imagine x does not establish that x can exist. To validly conclude that world (a) is better than world (b), we would have to know that world (a) is in fact possible; but this is precisely something we cannot know.

The fact that there is suffering in the world, then, is not proof that the God of mainline Christianity does not exist. The fact that there is suffering in the world is a mystery and a paradox, to be sure, but it is not a contradiction. If love by its very nature must be free, it is possible that, although God *allows* evil, he does not *will* it; and it is quite possible that he only allows it for the sake of some greater good.

(4) Is it possible that the good of love outweighs the evil of evil-doing and evil-willing?

Yes. There is reason to believe that the good of love trumps the evil of suffering or at least *will* at the end of time.

Whenever a couple marries, they give witness to the hope that it is at least possible that the love they have for one another will outweigh the challenges they will face. When they decide to have a child, the same is true. Is pregnancy comfortable? Is childbirth without pain? Is caring for a child easy? No. It involves suffering, and sometimes very great

suffering; but there is something that outweighs that suffering: love.

There are many ordinary examples of love outweighing
evil: sports victory after hard training, graduation and a job
after many years of study, success after failure, recovery after
surgery, and a clean house after a few hours of work. Of
course, someone might object, "but there are also many examples of evil outweighing love. There is defeat after hard
training, unemployment after many years of study (especially if one studies philosophy), and failure to recover after
surgery. Nevertheless, given that we cannot see all things,
there is reason to hope and believe that the good of love outweighs, or at least will outweigh, the evil of suffering.

(5) If God is all powerful, why does he not find some
other means to bring about the good of love?

Answer: perhaps there is no other means. Just as it is impossible to make a square circle, it is impossible to make an
act of authentic love without freedom. Rocks are not free.
When they help or harm, we do not claim that they hate or
love. Coffee is also not free. When it helps or harms, we do
not claim that it loves or hates. One may love or hate rocks
and coffee, but rocks and coffee do not love us (no matter
how much they may seem or don't seem to love us). As discussed above, love and freedom are interdependent. Freedom is a prerequisite for love.

(6) If there is no other means to bring about the good of love, doesn't it follow that God is not omnipotent?

If we accept the claim that there is no other way to bring about the good of love, it would seem to follow that there is something that God cannot do, and hence neither omnipotent nor worthy of the name "God".

One response to this question is to look at the definition of "omnipotent." To be omnipotent in any meaningful sense of the term is to be *capable of doing everything that can be done.* The strongest man on the earth cannot lift the island of Hawaii. It does not follow that he is not the strongest man on earth. The most brilliant genius cannot make a square circle. It does not follow that she is not the most brilliant genius. Likewise, God cannot make freedom (which is a prerequisite for love) unfree, but it does not follow that he is not all powerful. So long as one avoids defining "omnipotent" as "having the ability to do the impossible," it is not contradictory to hold that God is omnipotent even though love requires freedom and even though suffering can come from the misuse of freedom. Defining "omnipotent" as "having the power to do the impossible" is nonsense. It is a dead end. To do the impossible—to do that which cannot be done—violates the principle of contradiction and is utterly irrational. It is not paradoxical; it is contradictory and hence irrational.

What all this establishes, then, is that it is not inherently contradictory to hold that it is possible that an omnipotent, omniscient, and benevolent God exists.

Method Two

Another approach to the problem of evil—which is much simpler but much less intriguing and much more humbling—is to follow the example of Job. This approach involves acknowledging that suffering is ultimately a mystery and, hence, we cannot comprehend why God might allow suffering and evil. When Job, becomes overwhelmed with the mystery—which was made all the more overwhelming by the foolishness of his friends—God asks him numerous rhetorical questions: "Where were you when I laid the foundation of the earth? Tell me, if you have understanding. Who determined its measurements—surely you know! Or who stretched the line upon it? On what were its bases sunk, or who laid its cornerstone, when the morning stars sang together and all the sons of God shouted for joy? Have you comprehended the expanse of the earth? Declare, if you know all this." (Job 382-7; 18) These questions, though perhaps a bit insulting, drive the point home: Job is in no position to answer any of these questions much less fully resolve the problem of evil. Recognizing this, Job responds with intellectual and spiritual humility saying, "Behold, I am of small account; what shall I answer thee? I lay my hand on my mouth. I have spoken once, and I will not answer...." (Job 40: 4-5) Rather than becoming angry about his lack of understanding and God's touché, he embraces wisdom.

This humility is echoed later by Socrates, who was said to be the wisest man in Athens yet claimed to know nothing. Those who claim to have knowledge when they do not are suffering from self-deception. There is no wisdom in such deception, only foolishness and hubris. Those who know that they do not know and have the courage to admit it are those with true wisdom. It is not possible to fully resolve paradoxes, at least not if they are authentic paradoxes. But it is sufficient to show that they do not entail inherent contradictions. To be wise is to be able to distinguish between contradictions and paradoxes and acknowledge the fact that many paradoxes remain mysteries. To be foolish is to conclude that a paradox is a contradiction without having sufficient evidence. It is no coincidence that foolishness and hubris are frequently found together.

PARADOX OF THE FRUIT OF SUFFERING

"God comforts us in all our afflictions and thus enables us to comfort those who are in trouble, with the same consolation we have received from him. As we have shared much in the sufferings of Christ, so through Christ do we share abundantly in his consolation." (2 Cor 1:4-5)

There are many different types of suffering and there are many different types of fruit that can come from suffering. Suffering can be physical, existential, interpersonal, interior, psychological, moral, spiritual, and even demonic. It can stem from the sins of others, our own personal sins, and original sin. Such sins can include sins of omission and commission. Suffering can also stem from natural disasters, non-human causes, illnesses, and accidents. Sometimes, these can be foreseen, at other times they cannot. What is common to all types of suffering, however, is that they can bear fruit. And what is paradoxical is that good can come from suffering, regardless of its origin or type.

Physical suffering is very common and very obvious, but there are other types that are much more hidden—and for that reason sometimes even more difficult to bear. Existential suffering, or existential angst, is one such type, and it entails lacking a sense of meaning. As Nietzsche put it, and as Frankl frequently quoted, "He who has *a why* to live can bear with almost any *how*."[32] In other words, people can endure *anything*—even concentration camps—if they have a *reason* to endure such experiences or if they find some sort of meaning in such experiences. As a psychiatrist and survivor of Auschwitz, Frankl had ample exposure to human suffering. He had a front row seat to the inner turmoil of his own

---

[32] Viktor E. Frankl, *Man's Search for Meaning* (New York: Washington Square Press, 1984), 97.

suffering and that of others. He was by no means a stranger to suffering.

Years of research and experience led Frankl to conclude that what is most important for survival is having a sense of purpose. Many of his fellow prisoners took their own lives, but many more persevered. What those who persevered had in common was that they had a *why*, that is, they had a sense that their suffering was not in vain. Some persevered because they hoped to see their loved ones again. Others, because they had a sense that there was some mission or work they had yet to finish. Others, because they wanted to suffer well—heroically, courageously, virtuously, with dignity, and without being conquered by despair. And still others, because they wanted to prove that their captors could not triumph over them.

As a therapist, Frankl discovered that finding a sense of meaning in general and in relation to suffering was profoundly therapeutic. He developed a type of therapy, called logotherapy, which entailed helping his patients find a sense of meaning in their suffering. The following is an example of its fecundity. Frankl once had a patient who was suffering from severe depression and was overwhelmed with grief after having lost his wife two years earlier. Rather than giving him advice, Frankl simply asked, "What would have happened... if you had died first, and your wife would have had to survive you?" The man responded, "Oh...for her this would have been terrible; how she would have suffered!"

Frankl then said, "You see... such a suffering has been spared her, and it was you who have spared her this suffering—to be sure, at the price that now you have to survive and mourn her."[33] In this conversation, Frankl helped the man to find meaning in his suffering by helping him to realize he was no longer suffering in vain but suffering in place of his wife. It is for this reason that it became bearable to him. "In some way," Frankl noted, "suffering ceases to be suffering at the moment it finds a meaning, such as the meaning of a sacrifice."[34]

Frankl could have also pointed out to the man that had he not loved his wife he would not be in mourning. One mourns only, or at least primarily, when the departed is a loved one. Frankl could have asked the man if he would prefer not to be in mourning but to have never loved his wife, or to have loved his wife even though it now entailed suffering her loss. This also could have helped the man find a sense that his grief was not in vain.

Existential suffering is intense. We long for health, security, and sustenance but—given that we are rational creatures—we also long for meaning. Suffering from lack of a sense of meaning can be overwhelming, but it can nevertheless bear fruit if it spurs one on to find meaning. Existential angst is indeed a type of suffering, but it bears fruit when it

---

[33] Ibid., 135.

[34] Ibid.

is finally satiated. Just as physical hunger can bear fruit by spurring us on to eat, so, too, hunger for meaning can bear fruit by spurring us on to find meaning.

Another form of suffering is spiritual suffering. An example is the suffering which is a result of spiritual warfare. In *The Dialogue*, God the Father says to St. Catherine, "You see, then, that the demons are my ministers [sent] to… exercise and test your virtue in this life.[35] It is a startling revelation: God allows us to be tempted and harassed by the devil and his demons. It is not so startling, however, when we see that this suffering can bear great fruit. God does not will us to suffer at the hands of Satan for no reason, much less because he delights in the suffering of his servants. It is only for the sake of strengthening our virtue that he allows such suffering. It is often when we are most tempted against a virtue that we grow in it; and it is growth in virtue, not suffering, that God wills. Virtue is a habit, and like all habits they are acquired through repetition. It is precisely when we are tempted to despair, that we grow in hope; it is when we are tempted to be impure, that we grow in chastity; and it is when we are tempted to hate, that we grow in love. Just as a coach allows his trainees to experience the hardship and pain of training, but only for the sake of gaining strength and skill, so, too, God allows his saints to repeatedly experience the

---

[35] Catherine, of Siena. *The Dialogue* (New York: Paulist Press, 1980), section 43.

hardship and pain of temptation, but only for the sake of growth in holiness.

In his words to St. Catherine, God the Father makes it clear that when the devil tempts us against virtue it is not because the devil wills us to grow in virtue. The Father says, "[it] is not... the devil's intention to make you prove your virtue (for he has no charity). He would rather deprive you of virtue! But he cannot, unless you will it so."[36] The devil wills only our downfall and thus he "has no charity." God, on the other hand, wills our sanctity and so, though he allows us to suffer, it is only because he *has* charity. It is the fruit of suffering, not suffering itself, that God allows.

Another type of spiritual suffering—which was very well known by a great many mystics —is the dark night. We wounded humans are both sentient and intellective; we therefore need purification and healing of both our senses and intellect. Dark nights, though painful, can purify the soul in both ways. At the beginning stage of the spiritual life, it can be easy to equate God with sensate consolation. It may seem at first that God is nothing more than the felt sense of His presence which he sometimes gives us. "I love God," can sometimes means little more than: "I love the nice feelings I have when I am pious."

God loves us too much to allow us to equate our *experiences* of God with God himself. A rock in its fullness is always

---

[36] Ibid., 88.

far more than what we may perceive of it. Likewise, God in his fullness is always more than we perceive of him. He therefore withdraws the sense of his presence, not because he wills us to suffer, but because he wills that we come to a deeper knowledge of who he is. We cannot learn much about a rock from looking at it only from one side. So, too, we cannot learn much about God only by looking at the gifts he sometimes gives us.

The spiritual suffering which ensues from having God's felt presence withdrawn bears great fruit. Again, as with all suffering that God permits, it is for a greater good. God does not will his saints to feel far from him and suffer for the sake of suffering, but he does will that they come to a deeper knowledge of him and a more purified relationship with him. The sense of abandonment that God allows his saints to feel is a mere means to this. It is the fruit of suffering, not the suffering itself that God wills.

St. Catherine of Sienna wondered why God seemed to have abandoned her. In *The Dialogue,* God the Father asks, "Why do I keep this soul... in such pain and distress?" And he then responds, "not for her to be captured and lose the wealth of grace, but to show her my providence, so that she will trust not in herself but in me."[37] The fruit of St. Catherine's suffering was her recognition of God's providence and

---

[37] Ibid., 144.

a greater ability to humbly trust him. Her spiritual suffering bore great fruit and so, too, can ours.

The suffering of Christ on the cross bears witness to the fruit of suffering. Christ experienced a dark night of sorts when he suffered and died, but it was not because his relationship with his Father needed to be purified. The dark night of Christ has borne fruit in our lives by providing us with an example of how to suffer well and evidence that we do not suffer alone; we suffer with Christ.

Another type of suffering is that which emerges in interpersonal relationships. As is the case in our relationship with God, we often begin relationships with people because of the pleasure and rewards they bring us.[38] The classic example of this is found in romantic relationships in which the initial attraction is sparked by a desire for pleasure. Often, the initial desire is not for a deep and committed relationship—or what Aristotle calls a true friendship—but simply sexual pleasure or to have a "friend with benefits." Suffering in this type of case ensues if pleasure is not attained.

Likewise, we often begin relationships because we find them to be useful. Examples are legion: the employee builds up the ego of her boss in hope of a promotion, the man visits the Godfather only in hope of assistance in getting revenge against the man who assaulted his daughter, the elderly person butters up her neighbor only because she needs help.

---

[38] cf. Aristotle, *Nicomachean* Ethics.

Suffering in cases such as these ensues if the hoped-for assistance does not materialize.

There is no doubt that relationships with others entail suffering, yet this suffering can bear great fruit. We only come to have authentic, deep, and long-lasting friendship when we pass beyond being attracted to the other merely because he is pleasant and useful. A young man comes to a deeper relationship with his girlfriend precisely when he comes to love her for her sake and not for his own sake. This does not happen overnight, and it requires being purified from ulterior motives. Pagan though he was, Aristotle was able to see this. Perfect friendship, he said, was based on love the friend for the friend's own sake. (Ibid.) The purification which occurs in natural friendships, as the friends pass from self-love to authentic love of the other, can cause great suffering, but this suffering bears fruit when it blossoms into true friendship.

Yet another type of suffering is the suffering of martyrdom. The martyrs suffer torment and death, but in so doing they bear witness to Christ, provide others with inspiration, and bear witness to the fact that "love is as strong as death." (*Song of Songs* 8:6). This is true both of martyrs of faith and martyrs of love. It is also true of the witness of those who are persecuted for their faith even if they are not killed (especially since living martyrdoms can be even more painful than martyrdoms that result in death). Tertullian proclaims that martyrdom bears fruit when he says, "The blood of the martyrs is the seed of the Church." (*Apologeticus*, Chapter 50)

Let us look more closely at examples of the fruit of martyrdom. One of the many ways that martyrs bear fruit is by calling attention to the fact that there is more to life than mere survival and natural happiness, as well as by providing a profoundly strong example of steadfastness in faith. They can in so doing provide us with relief from our existential suffering. When we have trouble enduring the "how," the martyrs can provide us with a "why". We may say, "My life is hell and I cannot endure this. Why not just check out?" By their witness, the martyrs answer us by saying, "because suffering is only temporary, and it will not triumph. Love will!"

Similarly, those who die for their faith can inspire us to accept our daily white martyrdoms with greater patience and hope. We may ask: "Why must I put up with this insult or prejudice against me which I suffer on account of my faith? Wouldn't it easier just to hide myself away and be a closet Christian? Can't I believe in God and avoid the negative consequences?" The martyrs help us answer these questions and find the motivation to continue believing unabashedly. Faith can indeed be hard, and it often entails suffering. The martyrs bear fruit in our lives by saying, "Persevere, it will be okay. Do not be afraid."

Martyrs of love—those who die because of their charity or because they give their lives for others—also bear immense fruit. Our world is full of darkness, corruption, and indifference. It is easy to let this darkness blind us to the light. Martyrs of love give us hope for humanity and show us that people are capable of heroism. They show us that there are indeed people who have the greatest possible love and are willing to lay down their lives. (cf. John 15:13) In turn, they also bear witness to the truth that we, too, are called to heroic love. By their suffering they bear great fruit since by their suffering they inspire love and scatter the darkness.

St. Maximillian Kolbe is an excellent example of a martyr of love. He bore witness by his willingness to die for a fellow prisoner in Auschwitz. He did not come up with excuses. He did not say, "I ought to keep myself alive because, after all, I am a priest and cannot minister the Sacraments if I am dead." No, he ministered in the greatest way possible: by being a witness to perfect love and by following Jesus, the High Priest, to the Cross. Blessed Stanley Rother, and so many others, have done likewise. Their love was "stronger than death" in the most radical way possible. Their suffering bore fruit by bearing witness to love.

Moral suffering or "feeling the sting of conscience" is yet another type of suffering which can bear fruit. It is popular to point the finger at religion and moral codes and say, "They are oppressive, hypocritical, and leave people feeling guilty." It is likewise popular to embrace relativism and the claim that moral codes are merely random human inventions or conventions that do not have universal validity or relevance. Protagoras is frequently echoed: "Man is the measure of all things." (DK 80B1) Feelings of shame and guilt are often seen as unhealthy—a sign of depression or lack of self-esteem. Though it can sometimes be a sign of such things, it can often be a sign of health.

The sting of conscience can bear great fruit on both the natural and supernatural levels. On the natural level, it can play a pedagogical role. It is healthy for one to feel the sting when he or she has intentionally done something which has harmed others. The sting of conscience can teach us that something needs to change. Just as physical pain can alert one to the fact that something is wrong and that a doctor should be consulted, so, too, moral pain can alert one to the fact that something is awry. If a man feels guilty for driving drunk because he realizes he put himself and others at risk, this is a good thing. It is a sign of health. It is precisely guilt that might motivate him to make positive changes.

The sting can also bear fruit on the supernatural level. This can happen in a number of ways. First, it can happen insofar as it can enable one to see the need for mercy and the beauty of salvation. One who is always upright or who does not have a conscience will not be in a good position to recognize her need for forgiveness. It is when she recognizes her need for God's mercy that she is in such a position. As St. Paul reminds us, "God proves his love for us in that while were still sinners Christ died for us." (Romans 5:8) In like manner, moral suffering can put one in a good position to recognize just how blessed he is to be forgiven. It was only after recognizing his sinfulness that St. Augustine was able to see the greatness and profundity of Christ's love and to comprehend the Exultet: "O happy fault that earned for us so great, so glorious a Redeemer." Enduring the sting of conscience is what enabled St. Augustine and so many other sinners to find joy in Christ's forgiveness.

The sting can also help us grow in humility. When we do not fall or do not recognize our need for forgiveness, we can easily fall into the trap of thinking that we are self-sufficient and that we do not need to rely on God's grace. This is one of the greatest dangers in the spiritual life—to think we can go it alone. Moral suffering can bring us to an authentic self-knowledge and help us to "become like little children." (Matthew 18: 3) Little children know that they are not self-sufficient, and they have no shame when relying on others. We, too, are called to become like little children by acknowledging our neediness. It may be uncomfortable to feel ashamed and less than perfect, but it can nevertheless bear great fruit.

Finally, all types of suffering can bear fruit by enabling us to develop compassion for others. It is when I myself have been homeless that it is easiest to have compassion toward the homeless. It is when I myself have experienced alcohol addiction that it is easiest to have compassion on other alcoholics. In short, it is when I myself have suffered the same fate as my brothers and sisters, that I can truly suffer with them. It is for this reason that Mother Teresa wanted her Sisters to live in poverty. In order to serve the poor, to recognize oneself in the poor, to understand the poor, and to become truly empathetic toward the poor, it can be immensely helpful to have personal experience being poor.

It is true that suffering does not always bear fruit. It can make one stronger, yes, but it can also cripple. Nevertheless, it is a paradox and not a contradiction that suffering can and often does bear great fruit. This is a paradox in itself, and it is also a paradox which sheds light on other paradoxes such as the paradox of the passion of Christ and the paradox of evil as privation to which we now turn.

PARADOX OF EVIL AS PRIVATION

Evil has been defined by St. Augustine as a privation or corruption of the good. But it seems preposterous to claim that those things we consider to be evil (such as pain, death, disease, natural disasters, and sin) are mere privations. Anyone who is experiencing the evil of pain would be unconvinced if told that his pain is a mere privation of the good. Even if he was told that his pain is a privation of pleasure or of comfort, he would be unconvinced—and rightly so. Saying that evil is *not*, contradicts what is patently obvious: that evil *is*. It may seem, therefore, that St. Augustine's claim is a contradiction, not a mere paradox.

The seeming absurdity can be resolved by getting clear on what St. Augustine means. He does not simply claim that evil is a privation but rather that evil is a privation or corruption *of* measure, *of* form, or *of* order. He states, "Evil…is nothing else than corruption, either of the measure, or the form, or the order, that belong to nature. Nature therefore which has been *corrupted* is called evil."[39] Augustine makes the claim that everything that exists is either God or God's creation. Since God is good and since nothing would exist if it weren't for his creative action, all of his creation must be good in some sense. In other words, existence, whether it is God or a creation of God, is good by the very fact that it *is*. According to Augustine, if there was something that was completely evil, it would simply *not be* and, hence, nothing that *is* can be entirely evil.

Augustine clarifies his claim stating, "A bad measure, a bad form, a bad order, are either so called because they are less than they should be, or because they are not adapted to those things to which they should be adapted."[40] Let us look at some specific examples.

Examples of *lack of measure* that Augustine provides include doing less than one should, doing more than one should, doing something that should not be done at all, or doing something in a way that is unfitting or inconvenient.[41]

---

[39] Augustine, and Vernon J. Bourke, *The Essential Augustine* (New York: New American Library, 1964), p. 49ff. Emphasis mine.

[40] Ibid.

[41] Ibid.

Specific examples could include laziness, workaholism, being a helicopter parent, gluttony, murder, and adultery.

Examples of *lack of form* that Augustine gives include comparative ugliness, uncomeliness, and contextual unsuitability. The example he gives of unsuitability is public nakedness. Though it is suitable to go naked while bathing, it is not ordinarily so in public. Specific examples of uncomeliness could include foul language, being disrespectful to authority, and failing to adhere to basic social norms. And specific examples of comparative ugliness might include playdough in comparison to a Michelangelo statue or a decaying flower in comparison to a fresh one.

In regard to *lack of order*, Augustine gives the broad examples of improperly ordering things and ordering things less than they should be ordered. In discussing his hierarchy of being, he claims that the human soul is inferior to God but superior to the body. He also defines sin as a disorder or a "turning away (*aversion*) from the most-worthy Creator and a turning toward (*conversion*) the inferior things God has created."[42] It is important to emphasize that St. Augustine does not claim that anything is intrinsically evil. The sinner is a creature of God and is therefore good. Likewise, that which the sinner chooses is good insofar as it is created by God. Sin is choosing in a dis-ordered way. Lust, for example, is choosing sensual pleasures in such a way that it causes one

---

[42] Ibid., p. 45.

to turn away from God, gluttony is choosing food in such a way that it causes one to turn away from God, and idolatry is choosing a creature or artifact over God. In short, sin is choosing things lower on the hierarchy of good while turning away from something higher on the hierarchy of good. It is not choosing things that are bad in themselves.

It is clear that Augustine's theory of evil as privation does not entail that claim that there is no evil *in any sense*. What he is claiming is that there is no *entity* or *substance* which is evil. As a Manichean, before his conversion to Catholicism, he thought there were two substances in the world: good and evil. Both of these substances were supposedly at war with one another (like Darth Vader and Luke Skywalker). This enabled Augustine to make sense of the problem of evil. Why is there evil in the world? Not because God is lacking in omniscience, omnipotence, or benevolence—and not because he doesn't exist—but because evil is at war with God and all that is good. In reading the writings of Plotinus, Augustine was able to grasp the idea of a non-corporeal substance and also the idea that sin is a disorder, privation, or corruption of a substance. Evil is not a thing, rather, evil is an accidental property of something which is good. He would not say that Darth Vader is intrinsically evil. He would say that Darth Vader is a creature of God—and therefore fundamentally good—who choses things that entail turning away from God and who thereby sins and brings much suffering upon himself and others. More specifically, he would say that Darth

Vader is good but that he chooses lesser goods when he should choose higher goods. He chooses himself and his ego when he should choose love and self-transcendence.

How might we implement Augustine's theory of evil? Does it account for physical evil, such as sickness, death, broken bones, and pain? Does it account for moral evil, such as murder, theft, lust, narcissism, pride, and apostasy? Does it account for natural disasters?

It does. Augustine is not claiming that such evils do not exist at all but that they exist insofar as they relate to something else. Sickness is a lack of health and a disorder within one's physiology. Death is a corruption of the body and a lack of life. Broken bones are a perversion of what is supposed to be the case or, in other words, it is a lack of physical integrity of the bone.

As has been illustrated above moral evil or sin can be accounted for in terms of privation or, more specifically, a disordered will. In addition to lack of order, moral evil can also be accounted for in terms of a lack of proper form and measure. Pride is esteeming oneself too much. Greed is esteeming things of the world too much. Lust is esteeming the erotic in an improper context. Envy is esteeming another's property or circumstances too much.

Physical evils, such as natural disasters, can also be accounted for in terms of a lack of measure, form, and order. Disasters such as hurricanes (which are not evil in themselves) are evil insofar as they cause suffering. There is undoubtedly horrible weather on planets that have no life on them, but we do not call that weather evil. A drought on Mars or an ice-age on Neptune are not evil. The reason we call natural disasters on planet earth evil is that they can cause suffering, and suffering, in turn, can be accounted for in terms of privation and disorder. There is no need to postulate the existence of an evil substance, or to conclude that there is no God, in the traditional theistic sense, in order to acknowledge the gravity and presence of evil in the world.

It is worth noting that natural disasters can also sometimes be linked to moral evil. We are discovering more and more just how much certain types of human behavior can influence the environment in negative ways. These types of human behavior are often themselves sinful—though it is often difficult to see this connection. A child in a third world country may be starving due to a drought; the drought itself may be due to a change in weather patterns; the change in weather patterns may be due to an increase in carbon dioxide in the atmosphere; the increase in carbon dioxide may be due to excessive use of gas; the excessive use of gas might be due to inordinate use of motor vehicles; the inordinate use of motor vehicles might be due to the inordinate desire to consume; the inordinate desire to consume might be due to gluttony, avarice, pride, etc. It can be challenging to see how avarice and overconsumption can affect the environment, how that effect on the environment can be traced back to human behavior, and how changes in the environment can affect people in different parts of the world; yet, it is not impossible. Little by little we are coming to see how interlinked everything in the world is and how human behavior impacts others via the environment.

Thus, though St. Augustine's claim that evil is privation may seem to be patently absurd, at first blush, it is not. It is paradoxical, yes; but not contradictory.

Evil as a privation of empathy

God the Father's words to St. Catherine: "...lack of charity for me and for your neighbors is the source of all evils, for if you are not doing good you are necessarily doing evil." (*The Dialogue*, section 6)

With St. Augustine's privation theory of evil as a backdrop, let us consider empathy. One of the things that makes humans human is empathy, compassion, and sympathy. Hardened criminals are often referred to as inhuman, monsters, and beasts. Regardless of whether this is meant in a literal or merely metaphorical way, criminals indeed lack something. Is Hannibal Lector the ideal human? How about Hitler, Stalin, or Pol Pot? What is it precisely that they lack? The answer is empathy.

Sociopaths have one thing in common—they lack empathy. Part of being human is being able to feel with others, commiserate with others, put oneself in another's shoes, show compassion, and so on. When empathy is lacking, many things can go awry. It is precisely when a person does *not* have empathy that he can torture another human being without being affected by it. It is precisely when a person *does* have empathy that he cannot torture another—at least not without feeling that something is terribly wrong. People often ask the question, "How do these monsters sleep at night?" If indeed they do sleep at night, without having any qualms about their behavior, the answer is: they don't have empathy.

Much moral evil stems from lack of empathy and thus finding ways to foster empathy in ourselves and in others might go a long way toward reducing evil in the world. However, this leads to a new question: can empathy be fostered and, if so, how? In order to answer this question, it will be helpful to look at various types of lack of empathy.

There are four basic types of lack of empathy (1) involuntary and malignant, (2) involuntary and innocuous, (3) voluntary and referential, and (4) voluntary and dissociative. The first two types entail an *incapacity* to feel empathy. The lack of empathy, in these cases, is not voluntary and therefore the agents with this type of lack of empathy are not morally culpable. The second two types entail intentional lack of empathy and for this reason agents with this type of lack of empathy are morally culpable.

Examples of the first type can include serial killers, serial rapists, and sadists. Such persons are in many cases involuntarily lacking in empathy. For whatever reason, their brains are structured in such a way that they cannot imagine what it is like to be the victim. A perfect fictional character is Hannibal Lector. He does not feel remorse or have an inner sense that there is something deeply amiss about his behavior. He calmly bludgeons the prison guard to death and then goes on to enjoy his gourmet dinner and fine music. Nonfictional characters could include Gacey and Dahmer.

Examples of the second type of involuntary lack of empathy include Phineas Gage and people with certain types of autism. Due to a tragic accident, which sent a railroad pole through the frontal lobe in his brain, Phineas Gage became unempathetic. Before the accident he was a morally upright person, but after the accident his behavior changed radically. He did not become a sociopath nor pose a danger to others, but he was not the same conscientious, responsible, and upright person he was before. Some people on the autism spectrum similarly lack empathy.

The third type is voluntary lack of empathy, and it entails referring one's own guilt to that of another or, in other words, passing the moral buck to someone else. Such persons have the capacity to empathize with others, but they choose to blame the consequences of their actions on another person or organization. Many try to justify their heinous deeds by claiming, "I was doing my duty." How does the Nazi soldier justify systematic torture and murder of thousands of people? By convincing himself that it was his duty. This type of lack of empathy does not entail outright apathy, but it does entail some element of such a lack. Rather than having empathy for the victim, those who pass the moral buck convince themselves that the victim's suffering is a result of the commander's orders. There is enough suspension of empathy that the "obedient" man goes through with the harmful act.

The fourth type entails a splitting of one's personality or a dissociation from empathy which is initially present. Simply put, it involves lying to oneself (either consciously or subconsciously) and ignoring feelings of empathy that are present. "How do you sleep at night? How do you do what you do and then continue as if nothing happened?" The answer for many is, "I separate my work personality from my authentic personality." It does not require one to have clinical dissociative identity disorder, and indeed those who use this method to justify their heinous deeds most likely do not have a clinical disorder. It is not a clinical disorder but a moral disorder. One must first realize that what he is doing is wrong before he will have the need to utilize this defense mechanism. It does not require a lack of capacity for empathy, but it does require a moral dissociation. Those who use this mechanism are not true sociopaths, but they find a way to detach themselves from their empathy.

One way in which people can come to have a voluntary lack of empathy, or lack of conscience, is through repeatedly ignoring empathetic feelings and tendencies. Sometimes, this in turn can stem either from fear, uncertainty about how to respond, selfishness, self-centeredness, or some combination of these. One may, for example, feel a sense of empathy for a handicapped person and turn away out of fear. This turning away can stem from shock (for example, the handicapped person may be disfigured and awkward to look at). It can also stem from fear which in turn may stem from insecurity or shyness.

Sometimes, a person has empathy but simply does not know how to respond. Such a person may deliberate with himself saying, "Am I really helping this person by giving money? If so, is it more charitable and compassionate to do nothing? Is it even *possible* to help this person? By what means might I help this person? Do I have access to this means? Gosh, I don't know. But the light has just turned green, so I'd better just go." In the future, such a person might not even look at those who are in need and simply become indifferent. He may say to himself, "If I help this person in front of me, there will just be another such person tomorrow and the next day. I can't help everyone every day, so my policy is just not to worry about any of it." Through such self-talk one's empathy can atrophy until there is nothing left of it.

Selfishness and self-centeredness can also be a contributing factor. One may feel empathy but then quickly turn to his own needs as a means of looking away. One must look in some direction or other. If it is too uncomfortable to look in a particular direction, the easy solution is to avert one's eyes. "I would like to help this person but I'm very busy; I need to get to the store to buy paper towels. It would be imprudent to stop and go out of my way to help this person in need. After all, I might spill something during dinner tonight. So off to the store I go." Often, such petty voluntary dissociation from one's empathy does not kill empathy; nevertheless, it can weaken one's will and make it easier to dissociate the next time one is confronted with such situations. This type of apathy is voluntary—at least at the outset—even if it eventually kills empathy altogether.

There are many reasons why people are apathetic; and we now live in a world in which there is, as Pope Francis calls it, a "globalization of indifference." (*Laudato Si*, 52) Apathy is so widespread that it often goes unnoticed. Since there is nothing unusual about it, it seeps through the cracks and becomes more and more parasitical. It can end up draining us of life without our even realizing it.

Some Solutions:

Paradoxical as it may be, lack of empathy is at the heart of the problem of evil and thus growth in empathy can be part of the solution. This leaves us with one of the most urgent questions: how can we grow in empathy? The question is obviously not easy to answer but following are possibilities:

1. Raise Awareness.

There is no problem worse than one which is unrecognized. The first step to solving a problem, therefore, is to realize that there is one. When cancer is not identified, it can metastasize until it becomes fatal. What seems like a simple problem, a small melanoma on the skin, can lead to death if not promptly diagnosed and treated. Lack of empathy is no different. Without the awareness that lack of empathy is part of the problem, there is little chance that one will see the relevance of developing it in oneself or that of others. How often is it asked, "What is it to me? *Am I my brother's keeper?*" (Genesis 4:9)

This may seem like a very trite part of the solution. Saying, "just be empathetic" and "please recognize the problem" seems pointless. But voices crying in the wilderness can be great catalysts.

2. Enkindle Hope.

Raising awareness in itself, though necessary, not sufficient. In fact, if raising awareness is done in isolation from enkindling hope, it can even be harmful and deaden what empathy one has. It is easy to fall into thinking that problems are so big that it is useless to work toward solutions. Thus, raising awareness is only the first step. The second step is to recognize that the problem has a solution and that, even though it may be a world-wide problem that will require a world-wide response to solve, one's own personal behavior is relevant. One person is a drop of water, but the ocean is made up of drops of water.

3. Develop Self- Empathy.

"Love others as you love yourself." (Matthew 22:39) Learning the importance of empathy starts with having empathy toward oneself. Only when one loves oneself and sees oneself a worthy of empathy can one fully love others and see others as worthy of empathy. It is far easier to see others as *persons* when one recognizes one's own personhood. A person is not a thing, not an *it*. A person is a living, breathing, sensate being who has hopes, longings, and needs. A person is also a needy being who cannot live without others. No person is self-sufficient, and it is part of personhood to be needy.

Here's a thought experiment. Think of all the many things one does during the day that require reliance on others. Getting out of bed requires having a bed, having a bed requires others—the mattress designers, the mattress makers, mattress salespersons, and the mattress deliverers. So, in a sense, one cannot even get out of bed without implicitly relying on others. Taking a shower requires others. There are the shower designers, the shower makers, the welders, the shower installers, the plumbers. So, in a sense, one cannot take a shower without relying on others. Eating breakfast, doing errands, getting an education, getting a job, support-ing a family—none of this is possible without reliance on others.

Everybody is needy. Even the very wealthy are not self-sufficient. This is the case on a physical level but is equally, if not more, the case on a social level. As Aristotle wisely noted, "Without friends, no one would choose to live, even if he possessed all other goods."[43] And similarly, "He who is una-ble to live in society or who has no need because his is suffi-cient for himself, must be either a beast or a god."[44] There is a natural neediness in every heart that can only be fulfilled by the other. This is part of the essence of the human person.

Recognizing our own neediness can in turn help us to recognize the neediness in others. Just as I am needy and just as I must rely on others, so, too, my brothers and sisters are needy and must rely on others—including me. In other words, just as I need others to come to my assistance, so, too, others need me to come to their assistance. When I recognize that I am not the only one with needs, and when I recognize that others need me, I am in a good position to recognize that I have something to offer. I recognize that my own action or inaction has an effect on others even though, at first glance, this may not seem to be the case.

---

[43] *Nicomachean Ethics*, 8.1.1155a8-9

[44] *Politics*, 1.2.1253a28-30.

4. Educate for Empathy.

Education is one of the main keys to developing empathy. Tragically, education in individualistic societies often does little to foster empathy and develop other-oriented attitudes. Children are taught to share, to avoid littering, and not to hit. But children often are not given the tools necessary to identify with others, especially with those they may see as inferior. It is a bold endeavor to strive to teach children empathy, but it is of utmost importance.

It has been argued that empathy cannot be taught, and it is therefore tempting to despair. This despair, however, is part of the problem. As discussed above, some people are—for whatever reason—unable to experience empathy. It does not follow, however, that striving to educate children for empathy is futile.

Methods for teaching empathy can include using film and literature in order to give children a sense of what it is like to have specific challenges. By being immersed in the story lines of others, it becomes possible to gain deeper insight into the joys and sorrows of those we might not otherwise be able to identify with. I was not born blind or deaf but by reading about Helen Keller I can come to have a glimpse of what it would be like. I did not experience the Jewish Holocaust, but by reading *Diary of Anne Frank* or *Man's Search for Meaning*, I can again come to have a glimpse of what it would be like. There are oodles of works of literature, films, biographies, poems, and songs that can be used to provide children with opportunities to grow in understanding and compassion. Combining the reading of such works with opportunities for self-reflection could be effective.

Immersion in the stories of others and opportunities for self-reflection are only first steps. Children also need to be given a sense of empowerment. What good does it do to feel compassion toward others if it leads to nothing but an increase in sorrow and a sense of powerlessness? Simply feeling compassion toward others can, in some cases, only serve to cause one to experience hopelessness. So, in addition to developing empathy in children, it is also necessary to provide them with ways to *express* that empathy, develop hope, and come to see how they can be a part of the solution. This, too, can be provided through film and literature. It is tempting to despair and think that all is lost, but when we hear of the lives of the Mother Teresas, the Catherine of Sienas, and the Malala Yousafzais, we can come to realize that there is hope and that we, too, can find ways to bring about positive change. Educating children in the ways of hope and solidarity is essential; and it is part of the practical solution to the problem of suffering, which we will return to shortly.

PARADOX OF
TRUTH LEADING TO FALSEHOOD

In *The Dialogue,* God the Father states, "For often the devil would make you see too much of the truth in order to lead you into falsehood."[45] What could this possibly mean? How is it possible that truth could lead one to falsehood? Isn't this a contradiction?

In the practical realm, it is possible for too much truth to lead to falsehood. When one looks at certain facts but fails to balance them with other facts, it is possible to become cynical or fall into despair. One may, for example, become intensely overwhelmed by the fact that he has failed in some way. It may be financial failure, failure in one's profession, failure in love, moral failure, athletic defeat, or any other type of failure. When one becomes too intensely focused on his failure, he may conclude that he is *nothing but* a failure. This in turn may lead to giving up, becoming despondent, becoming scrupulous, or even something as dramatic as suicide.

Is it true that people sometimes fail miserably in romance? Certainly. Is it true that people fail morally, even to a significant extent (perhaps by killing someone in an act of passionate revenge)? Unfortunately, yes. There is no doubt that these types of things happen frequently. There is also no doubt that these kinds of things lead people to think they are

---

[45] *The Dialogue,* section 102.

lost, unforgivable, unlovable, beyond hope, or even subhuman. But does is it therefore true that people who fail are in fact unforgivable, beyond hope, subhuman? Fortunately, no. Facts can and do often lead people to make false conclusions. Too much of one type of truth, considered in isolation from other facts, can lead one into falsehood.

In the abstract realm, it is also possible for truth—or partial truth—to lead to falsehood. This often happens when facts are taken out of context. This can even happen in the seemingly objective realm of statistics. It is a fact that there the human population has risen at a startling rate in the past two centuries. It is a fact that there is a lack of resources and space in many parts of the world which stems from overpopulation. Does it follow that there is a worldwide lack of space or resources? Are we justified in concluding that because there has been an exponential increase of population there will only be an arithmetical increase in resources? Many have concluded "yes." Yet, these conclusions are not justified and in fact we can now see that these conclusions were inaccurate. Though there is overpopulation in certain regions, there is more than enough space available for humans to dwell. Though there has been an explosion in terms of population, it does not follow that there is a worldwide lack of resources. One cannot look at the truth that there is a food shortage in one region and conclude that there is a worldwide food shortage. Perhaps if sustainable farming and fishing were to be taught and implemented, the food shortage

would subside. Perhaps if the importance of sharing resources were to be more widely known and encouraged, the
food shortage would subside even more. We simply cannot
look at one particular region and make the conclusion that
what is true of that region is true of all regions. Moreover,
from the fact that one type of solution is effective in one particular region, we cannot conclude that the solution will necessarily always work in all regions and without negative side-
effect.

Partial truth can lead to false conclusions. It would therefore be helpful to revise the statement of St. Catherine to say:
too much truth *in isolation* from other truths can lead to
falsehood, and too much truth *taken out of context* can lead
to falsehood. Truth in isolation from other truths and truths
taken out of context can lead to actions that make things
even worse. Evil can easily seep in where it is least expected.
Evil is often subtle.

TWO PARADOXES REGARDING SOLUTIONS TO THE PROBLEM OF EVIL

I. The problem of evil is abstract, but the solution is both abstract *and* practical

The problem of evil is obviously an abstract, theoretical,
philosophical, and theological problem. It is true, even if

uncomforting, that this syllogism implicitly if not explicitly echoes in the minds of many:

(1) If God exists, there will be no suffering.
(2) There is suffering.
(3) Therefore, God does not exist.

Given that the syllogism is valid, and the premises may seem to be true, the logician is right to acknowledge that the problem has a theoretical basis. The logician is also right to tell the believer of a perfect God that he (the believer) bears the burden of proof. Furthermore, the logician is right to point out to the believer that he needs to establish that one, or both, of the premises are false if he is to make any progress in solving the problem.

As we have seen, there are many abstract ways of establishing that premise one is not self-evident. What is paradoxical, however, is that the problem of evil requires both abstract and practical solutions. It may seem absurd or contradictory to claim that an abstract problem requires a practical solution. Indeed, to claim that an abstract problem can have a practical solution may seem as absurd as to claim that a mathematical problem can be solved with a light bulb.

So how can it be that the problem of evil can have a practical solution? How can it be that the ivory tower can have anything to do with the highways, byways, and dirty streets of the slums? In order to answer these questions, let us look more closely at premise one: if there is a perfect God, there will be no suffering.

In the streets and slums, it is obvious that there is suffering. People are starving, living without hope, dying of injuries and diseases, being exploited in horrific ways, and despairing of ever finding a way out. In the streets and slums, it is also obvious, however, that the actions and inactions of people greatly contribute to this suffering. Speak to the injured woman. Ask her how she was injured. She may respond, "My husband hit me" or "A drunkard ran a red light and crashed into my car." Then ask the crying child, "Why are you crying?" She might say through her sobs, "Because my father is dying and because I am hungry." Then ask the beggar, "Why do you beg?" She may respond, "Because my child is dying, and I cannot afford to take her to the doctor." Then ask her, "Why don't you get on Medicaid?" She may respond, "There is no such thing in my country. If you can't pay the doctor at the outset, he will not treat you."

There are many such slums but if it seems unrealistic, go to another. Ask the woman, "Why are you injured?" She may respond, "Because I was drunk and fell down the stairs." Ask the child, "Why are you crying?" She might say, "Because I got mad, hit my brother, and he then hit me back." Then ask the beggar, "Why do you beg? Why don't you get a job?" He may say, "Because it's easier to beg than to work. You see, I am just too lazy to work."

In the first slum, you will find people suffering because of the actions and inactions of others. In the second slum, you will find people suffering (arguably) because of the consequences of their own actions and inactions. In neither slum, however, will you find evidence that the people suffer because there is no God; or that they suffer because God is not perfect. Through personal experience, one can come to see first-hand that it is quite possible that, even if God were perfect, people might still suffer on account of their own actions and inactions. The street might have something to say to the ivory tower after all.

In addition to helping one come to see that people, not God, are the source of much suffering, the streets can also help one come to see his or her *own* place in the scheme of things. On the street, one may see an injured woman and then remember, "I myself hit her" or "I let her drive while intoxicated." One may see a crying child and then remember, "I never gave that child food." One may see the beggar and then realize, "I have never done anything to help the poor."

In the street, sometimes, the tables turn. Sometimes, *we* are injured and see the man who hit us. Sometimes, *we* are begging because we were thrown out. Sometimes, *we* are crying because someone stole from us. Sometimes, *we* are injured because of a drunk driver. When the tables turn, the experience can shed light on the abstract problem and can also enable us to see that a practical solution, even if not the entire solution, is necessary.

Finally, the streets can help show us that we can become part of the solution through practical acts of concrete love in daily life. "How can I help this injured woman?" By taking her to the hospital. "How can I help this crying child?" By feeding him. "How can I prevent this young man from becoming a beggar?" Educate him. "How can I bring about more joy in the lives of others?" By loving them.

A practical solution cannot, in itself, annihilate the abstract aspect of the problem. Even if all people suddenly had heroic charity, there would still be suffering in the world (at least at the outset until the charity had time to bring about a full healing). So long as there is suffering in the world, there will always be a longing in the minds of many for an abstract solution. So long as there is suffering in the world, people will have difficulty swallowing the notion of a perfect God. Nevertheless, striving to implement practical solutions can shed light on the abstract problem. A lightbulb cannot solve a math problem, but it can provide the light necessary for the mathematician to solve it. It is the light of practicality that sheds light upon the fact that the first premise may be wrong. It is the light of practicality that can help us see that it is our own actions, and the actions of others, that brings about so much suffering—not God.

II. Solutions are sometimes problems

Another paradox regarding solutions to the problem of evil is that supposed solutions can often be part of the problem. It often seems patently obvious that to fix a problem within a system, it is sufficient to find the malfunctioning part and fix it. In simple mechanical systems, such as watches, it is very effective to fix one part in order to make the system work again. Replace a dead battery with a good battery, and the watch works again.

However, when applying this principle to more complex systems (such as legal systems, interpersonal relationships, the ecosystem, and the muscular-skeletal system), applying this principle can be ineffective and even counterproductive. Fixing one problem without considering the whole can end up setting off a domino effect which ends up making things worse in the end. Take for example, trash. Trash is a problem. Nobody wants it at their doorstep. So, off to the landfill it goes… and goes… and goes. As it goes, the problem at our doorstep goes with it… but eventually it will come back in some way, either in our own lives or in the lives of others and future generations. Present-day solutions are often nothing more than tomorrow's problem.

Transportation is another example. The human race is always in need of transport and without it problems cannot be solved. To solve the problem of hunger, we need to go to the store. To solve the problem of illness, we need to go to the doctor. It is obvious, of course, that transportation solves many problems—yet it is now becoming more and more obvious that it is also causing problems. Moreover, it is now becoming obvious that it can cause the very things it is supposed to solve. One goes to the hospital to look for a cure for emphysema and on the way emits toxins which can cause emphysema.

Human trafficking is yet another example. An increase in production leads to an increase in profit, and an increase in profit can solve many problems. With more money, there is more access to health care, with more access to health care, people are healthier. Yet an increase in production can also paradoxically come at the expense of the most vulnerable: children who are forced to fish in dangerous situations for twelve or more hours a day, and young women and girls who are used as machines in garment factories and as objects in brothels. Production solves problems, and cheap production solves even more problems (at least from the perspective of the pocket liners). In seeing these instant "solutions," however, it can become more and more difficult—sometimes even impossible—to see the big picture. And it is the big picture that often reveals to us that the "solution" is creating more problems than it actually solves. Cheap production and quick money-making solve many problems *for a few people,* but it may come at the price of the exploitation of *the many.*

There is no linchpin solution. Though it is tempting, it is not wise to point to one aspect and say, "See, here is the problem. Fix it and the problem will be gone." No, the problems we face are multifaceted, so the solution must also be. We are physical, spiritual, communal, intellective (at least sometimes), consumptive, sexual, and interdependent, political beings. If my physical well-being is compromised, it may compromise my communal relationships. Thus, in order for true and lasting solutions to be found, all aspects of human life and the environment must be considered. There is need for change on every level. It is indeed a profoundly difficult task, but it is one which is urgent and essential.

As Pope Francis has pointed out, it is essential that we avoid trying to solve problems in isolation from the whole. He admonishes us to consider whether human interventions are actually solving problems or just further aggravating them. He calls for a change in our current "technocratic paradigm" which blindly accepts advances in technology "without concern for its potentially negative impact on human beings."[46] There is a need not merely for problem solving, but also for an analysis of the problem-solving techniques we employ. Ultimately, this requires a transformation of mind and heart.

One of the most illuminating examples Pope Francis gives is our attitude toward consumption. It seems harmless to buy, sell, use, and enjoy products. Yet, it is only harmless if done in proper proportion and with awareness of the con-

---

[46] *Laudato Si*, 109.

sequences. We tend to place priority not on *being* but on *being useful.*[47] We tend to see things as having value only if they can be consumed and used. This attitude, however, can affect our overall mindset including our relations with others. It is not far-fetched to see that a utilitarian attitude toward the world is the fundamental attitude toward those who are involved in sex trafficking. If I see the world as something to be used, I will be able to also see human beings as things to be used. It is a travesty that human beings are bought, sold, and consumed as if they were mere objects.

Thus, nothing can be excluded from consideration when looking for solutions to problems. There is no single cause, so there is no single solution. All must be put on the discernment table: actions, inactions, attitudes, behavior, the spiritual, the physical, the psychological, the environment, animals, plants, and even dirt. Everything in the intricate system in which we live is relevant.

That solutions can sometimes cause problems, even the very problems the solutions seek to solve, is paradoxical but not contradictory. Illumination and recognition of this paradox is essential if we are to find authentic and long-lasting solutions.

To summarize, there are many paradoxes of good and evil. The problem of evil in regard to God can only be solved by considering the nature of evil and relating it to human

---

[47] Ibid., 69.

action and inaction. Acknowledging and illuminating these paradoxes is essential in bringing about the good. Ignoring them or casting them aside as contradictions only allows evil to triumph.

CONCLUSION

Grappling with paradoxes is part of the human condition. Looking at them in the eye and seeing them for what they are can be utterly terrifying. Yet, it is the only authentic way to grow as humans if—as has been proclaimed by many a saint and sage—humans are rational, questioning animals.

Some upon seeing paradoxes, uncritically conclude that they are contradictions and abandon further pursuit. Others upon seeing them, choose to look away and give into cowardice or denial. After all, honest enquiry requires courage and perseverance. Others, upon seeing them, rouse up enough courage look at them but then despair of ever finding answers. Atheism, agnosticism, skepticism, and apathy in general are all symptoms of such despair.

But others, upon seeing paradoxes, choose to dig into them long enough and courageously enough to discover that the seeming contradictions can often be illuminated. It is for such as these that faith and hope become possible.

In your light, oh Lord, we see light. You are a mystery, but you are also the Logos. Grant us courage, hope, and grace that we may seek you through faith and reason with all our heart, soul, mind, and strength. Amen.

Made in the USA
Middletown, DE
02 June 2022